What Hath

Eve

Wrought?

or

W.H.E.W.!

What Hath Eve Wrought? or W.H.E.W.!

Marilyn M. Adams

authorHOUSE®

AuthorHouse™
1663 Liberty Drive
Bloomington, IN 47403
www.authorhouse.com
Phone: 1-800-839-8640

First published by AuthorHouse   09/07/2011

ISBN: 978-1-4634-4674-1 (sc)
ISBN: 978-1-4634-4673-4 (ebk)

Library of Congress Control Number: 2011914131

Printed in the United States of America

Prologue

I do not recall what book devoted to the nineteenth century feminist pioneers awakened my cloistered desires for personal freedom, but I do vividly remember being severely chastised for reading "evil literature." That denunciation of my choice of reading material fired my interest in learning about the suffragists who fought for the equality that was legally withheld from all women. Fortunately, my newly discovered ability to voice my independent thoughts led to divorce. I was now free to become what, I suppose, I was always meant to be. The year was 1985; I was 59 years old.

I had vague recollections of the rebirth of feminism in the 1960's, but that decade had been my rebirth as well, leading me back to academia, to the studies I had abandoned years before. Domestic circumstances then seemed to dictate the necessity of obtaining a degree to enable me to support my two children since their welfare and their educational future would soon be my responsibility and mine alone. Within the space of four years, I acquired two degrees from UCLA; then received my first teaching assignment. But when I retired from the scholastic environment fifteen years later, I foolishly embarked on another marital adventure. Almost five years later, my fortunate foray into forbidden literature set me free. I could indulge in the history of a movement of which I had just become aware. I believed that somehow I could bring the words and deeds of the nineteenth century feminists, the stalwart precursors in the lengthy battle for woman's equality, to life. Therefore, as I read their words, written and spoken, I saved them for future use, not knowing just how I could present them to an audience of readers or listeners. I also discovered the anti-suffragists, the anti-equality men whose pronouncements from pulpit or their denunciations in print relegated all women to a subservient position because of the supposed "sin" of the mythical Eve. Their words, too, I determined, were necessary to demonstrate the long-held fear of woman's clamor for equality.

Susan B. Anthony eventually became my *alter ego*. Her words that I had culled from quotations collected for years blossomed into a one-woman show that I performed as a Chautauqua Scholar under the auspices of the New Mexico Humanities Council in some forty venues throughout the state. Soon I also used the words of many other nineteenth century feminists, scripting their speeches and writings into a theatrical production entitled *An Improper Woman* that included the comments from an array of male antagonists.

In the late 1990's, I discovered a recently published history of pro-feminist men, edited by Michael S. Kimmel and Thomas E. Mosmiller. Entitled *Against the Tide, Pro-feminist Men in the United States 1776-1990*, it is a compilation of speeches, essays and actions by men who did not fear women as equal partners, who braved the taunts and jeers of the male majority. I soon added another one-woman show to introduce some of these pro-feminist, pro-suffragist men who had been a vital component of the lengthy battle for woman's equality: *A Male Minority: Men Who Stood with Women for Equality.*

The religious fervor of the early decades of the nineteenth century placed emphasis on the Biblical account of creation, on the story of Eve's disobedience, her sin against God. It was held then that all women, as her descendants, had the same willful disposition and must be held in subjection to the superior male. Therefore, the battle for the equal rights of female citizens was an uphill fight. And what Eve hath wrought became a crucial component of that struggle. It was, I knew, truly an epic story that could be presented in the actual words of the combatants. Their voices, male as well as female, might serve as an essential complement to history text books that for generations have omitted the vital dramatic episodes culminating in the passage of the Nineteenth Amendment to the Constitution of the United States. Therefore, *What Hath Eve Wrought?* or, acronymically titled *W.H.E.W.!*, is my legacy, my desire to impart some accounting of the seemingly unending battle for woman's equality.

Myth and Consequences

It was Eve who precipitated the fall of man and caused the loss of peaceful, carefree Eden. It was she who, in league with Satan, disobeyed God, tempted Adam and, by this flagrant deed, proved herself and, therefore, all women, in perpetuity, dangerous, cunning, easily led astray and decidedly different from man, the superior being.

Having stated these sinister proclivities attributed to Eve, it is somewhat difficult to struggle with the logic which insists that the peace of Eden would have been the norm, that war and all its attendant horrors would have been unknown, that human nature would have remained without blemish in tune with the laws of God, that the lion would live in harmony with the lamb. That logic held that Eve, recalcitrant Eve, could be blamed for all the woes of the world.

A painful price was to be paid for Eve's indiscretion, a price to be suffered by all subsequent mothers. The agonies of childbirth were to be borne for evermore by all women, unlike the relative calm experienced by non-human females. It should also be noted, as a pertinent aside, that Eve seemed to be the only female in existence to produce future generations.

If the importance of a myth that clouds reason is not its factual basis, it is the message it contains. Honnor Martin wrote in 1898, a dissonant truth from the well-worn story:

Harken, O Eve, Mother of us all, greatest and grandest of women. You, who have been maligned all down the ages, know at least one of your daughters blesses you and proclaims your choice good. To you, O, Eve, we owe that we are not as gods and not as children playing in the garden—that we know the good and evil and are not lapst in ignorance and lust. Man would have stayed forever in uninquiring peace, but to you was given the strength to grasp the apple, to proclaim that woman, at least, prefers wisdom and the wilderness to idle lasciviousness in Eden.

Eve became every woman portrayed in physical and emotional negatives. The monthly loss of blood led to the belief that women were incapacitated and irrational when menstruating. Furthermore, at the onset of menopause, the inability to control sudden physical heat seemed to portend an age of witches and females engrossed in various forms of wickedness.

Avoiding outright mention of menstruation or other female mysteries, French historian Jules Michelet wrote concerning the physical differences of the human female in Woman's Love and Life, 1881:

Woman does nothing as we do. She thinks, speaks and acts differently. Her tastes are different from our tastes. Her blood even does not flow in her veins as ours does; at times it rushes through them like a foaming fountain torrent. She does not respire as we do. Making provision for pregnancy and the future ascension of the lower organs, nature has so constructed her that she breathes, for the most part, by the four upper ribs. From this necessity results woman's greatest beauty and gently undulating bosom which expresses all her sentiments by a mute eloquence. She does not eat like us—neither as much nor of the same dishes.

Why? Chiefly because she does not digest as we do. Her digestion is every moment troubled by one thing: she yearns with her very bowels. The deep cup of love (which is called the pelvis) is a sea of varying emotions hindering the regularity of nutritive functions.

Thomas A. Emmet, a renowned gynecologist, wrote in 1879, regarding the onset of womanhood: *To reach the highest point of physical development the young girl of the better classes of society should pass the year before puberty and some two years after free from all exciting influences . . . . Her mind should be occupied by a very moderate amount of study with frequent intervals of a few moments each, passed when possible in a recumbent position, until her system becomes accustomed to the new order of life.*

Marriage and child-bearing were obligatory for women who were, however, to behave as ladies. William Acton opined in his <u>Functions and Disorders of the Reproductive Organs,</u> 1875:

I should say that the majority of women (happily for society) are not much troubled by sexual feelings of any kind. Many of the best mothers, wives and managers of households know little or are careless about sexual relations. Love of the home, children and domestic duties are the only passions they feel. As a general rule, a modest woman seldom desires any sexual gratification for herself. She submits to her husband's embraces but primarily to gratify him and, were it not for the desire of maternity, would far rather be relieved from his attention.

Often, the degradation of woman is termed misogyny, the hatred of woman. I believe gynephobia, meaning fear of woman, was, and still is, the more accurate term. Gynephobia holds woman in thrall to ideas of male superiority that have been perpetrated throughout the centuries. It is the fear of the loss of male power and dominion, the spreading of allegations of what the unnatural power of woman would mean for society. It would usurp the "natural" power of men and demand equality in marriage; it would compel equality in education, in employment and wages; women would assume the male role in dress, wearing trousers (!); they would demand entrance into the military, desire religious offices. Foregoing their roles as mothers, wives and obedient daughters, leaving hearth and home, who would care for the children, the daily needs of the household? The whole idea of equality was, at best, ludicrous. Fear was manifested in ridicule, sarcasm and contempt.

Having exposed my readers to some of the opinions of the nineteenth century, I intend to give further quotations on the subject of woman's rights in the words of men who were decidedly in agreement with the status quo. But far less known are the words of the men who stood with women for equality. They have been largely forgotten and deserve to be resurrected and given the recognition due them. These are the men who realized the unfairness of woman's position and her limited opportunities. Most quotations cited are from the nineteenth century when the realization of a lack of freedom awakened a striving for fairness and opportunity for the status of women; when female education was considered unimportant, even dangerous; her choices in employment severely limited; her freedom non-existent under the law. Some quotations are from the eighteenth century and from the first years of the twentieth century. All, however, are intended to show that woman chafes under restrictions that degrade, subordinate, humiliate, control, confine, insult or enslave her. And, it is my contention that many of yesterday's wrongs, injustices and ensuing frustrations are still in practice today. Woman must still demand basic human rights to fulfill her need for human dignity.

The words of Louise Otto in 1849, are as vital in their content today and for years and perhaps decades to come:

The history of all times, and of today especially, teaches that . . . women will be forgotten if they forget to think about themselves.

A few gynephobic quotations seem appropriate now, starting with the words of the Emperor Napoleon who proclaimed in 1795:

Nature intended women to be our slaves . . . they are our property; we are not theirs. They belong to us just as a tree that bears fruit belongs to a gardener. What a mad idea to demand equality for women . . . . Women are nothing but machines for producing children.

German philosopher G.W.F. Hegal in 1820, made known his views on the consequences of giving women equality. His words also tread the gynephobic trail:

If women were to control the government, the state would be in danger, for they do not act according to the dictates of universality, but are influenced by accidental inclinations and opinions.

Male experts, producing their scientific findings, demonstrated their gynephobia when women were demanding equality in education. In 1873, Dr. Edward Clarke of the Harvard Board of Overseers wrote:

Identical education of the two sexes is a crime before God and humanity that physiology protests against and that experience weeps over.

An early twentieth century psychologist produced his views on the lack of intelligence of women. Apparently, Biblical authority for female subordination was confirmed or replaced by biological authority:

A woman's brain evolves emotion rather than intellect; and whilst this feature fits her admirably as a creature burdened with the preservation of the human species, it painfully disqualifies her for the sterner duties to be performed by the intellectual facilities. The best wife and mother and sister would make the worst legislator, judge and police officer.

S.P. Foster of Elmer, New Jersey, speaking for the average man of his time, wrote:

As a whole, women are utterly unfitted to pilot ships, command armies or operate automobiles through no fault of their own. They were born that way.

In 1911, Charlotte Perkins Gilman unearthed some choice comments:

Women were a sex; "the sex" according to chivalrous toasts; they were set aside for special services peculiar to femininity. As one scientist put it in 1888: "Women are not only the race, but a sub-species told off for reproduction only." The mental attitude toward women is even more clearly expressed by Mr. H.B. Marriot-Watson in his article The American Woman, 1903, where he says: "Her constitutional restlessness has caused her to abdicate those functions which alone can excuse or explain her existence."

Fear of the female then, seemed to be lurking in the cautionary words of male writers, speakers, philosophers, educators, churchmen, psychologists and other men of assorted speaking and writing abilities. They couched their fears in delineating woman's place in the scheme of the world as being the lesser part of humanity. And what better way to ensure male superiority than through the marriage bond.

Marriage was the occupation designated for all women. But when a woman married she lost what few rights she had had as a single woman. In 1854, Barbara Bodichon wrote <u>A Brief Summary in Plain Language of the Most Important Laws Concerning Women.</u> Although Bodichon was citing the laws of England, the same laws were practiced in the United States. These were the major elements:

- *A man and wife are one person in law and she loses all her rights as a person, and her existence is entirely absorbed in that of her husband. He is civilly responsible for her acts; she lives under his protection and cover, and her condition is called coverture.*
- *A woman's body belongs to her husband; she is in his custody, and he can enforce his right by a writ of habeas corpus.*
- *What was her personal property before marriage, such as money in hand, money at the bank, jewels, household goods, clothes, etc. becomes absolutely her husband's, and he may assign or dispose of them at his pleasure whether he and his wife live together or not.*
- *Money earned by a married woman belongs absolutely to her husband; that and all sources of income are included in the term personal property.*
- *By the particular permission of her husband she can make a will of her personal property, for by such permission he gives up his right. But he may revoke his permission at any time before probate.*
- *The legal custody of the children belongs to the father.*

Most states claimed another right for husbands: the right to hospitalize a wife for insanity with the asylum superintendent's approval, without going through any further medical or legal procedures to protect her rights. In Illinois, Elizabeth Parsons Ware Packard (1816-1897) married a Calvinist preacher who had her institutionalized in 1861, when she challenged the church doctrine he so fervently believed. The law stated:

Married women and infants who, in the judgment of the medical superintendent of the state asylum at Jacksonville, are evidently insane or distracted, may be entered or detained in the hospital at the request of the husband or guardian, without the evidence of insanity required in other cases.

The state law specified a two-year observation period before deciding whether a patient was curable or not.

Mrs. Packard spent three years in the state asylum before being released to her twenty-one year old son. But now her husband had her confined at home, locked in a small room with the window boarded, so she could not communicate with the outside world. She did find a way to slip a note through the closed window describing her predicament and asking for help. Eventually this led to a trial, involving false imprisonment at home and false imprisonment in an insane asylum. Was the conflict over Calvinist doctrine reason for Mrs. Packard's incarceration? Did women have the right to their own thoughts? After a dramatic trial, she was declared sane.

Now known as Mrs. E.P.W. Packard, she began a crusade to reform the laws that gave husbands the legal right to imprison their wives. She worked tirelessly for the rest of her life writing books and pamphlets, lecturing, lobbying in thirty-one states and was personally instrumental in changing attitudes toward the mentally ill and psychiatric treatments. Seldom remembered today for her persistent challenges to unfairness to women judged insane by their husbands, she, in her time, achieved prominence nationally.

In the 1880's, Emily Collins wrote about "domestic chastisement" in her memoirs:

In those early days a husband's supremacy was reinforced . . . by corporal chastisement, and it was considered both right and proper by most people as much so as in the correction of refractory children in like manner. I remember in my own neighborhood a Methodist class-leader and exhorter, deemed a worthy citizen who, every few weeks, gave his wife a beating with a horse whip. He said it was necessary in order to keep her in subjection and because she scolded so much.

In 1830, on Christmas morning, fifteen-year-old Elizabeth Cady was displaying her many gifts, among which were a coral necklace and bracelets. Henry Bayard, a family friend, commented:

Now, if in due time you should be my wife, those ornaments would be mine; I could take them and lock them up, and you could never wear them without my permission, I could even exchange them for a box of cigars, and you could watch them evaporate in smoke.

When Elizabeth Cady married Henry Stanton, they omitted the "obey" from their vows, just as Angelina Grimké and Theodore Weld had before them. Such an omission implied a wife could refuse to have intercourse with her husband—a difficult concept for most men to comprehend. Later Mr. Weld suggested that she combine her family and married names. He said, "Do not allow any of your correspondents to insult you by addressing your letters 'Mrs.

Henry B. Stanton.'" She considered and agreed. Later, when queried, she wrote:

I have serious objections . . . to being called Henry. Ask our colored brethren if there is nothing to a name. Why are slaves nameless unless they take that of their master? Simply because they have no independent existence. They are mere chattels with no social or civil rights. Even so with women. The custom of calling Mrs. John This or Mrs. Tom That and colored men Sambo or Zip Coon is founded on the principle that white men are the lords of all. I cannot acknowledge this principle as just; therefore, I have always referred to myself as Elizabeth Cady Stanton.

Amelia Bloomer commented on the same subject in her monthly magazine <u>The Lily</u> (1849-1855) which promoted suffrage, temperance, marriage law reform and higher education for women:

Why a woman as soon as she is married is willing to drop the good name of Mary or Elizabeth and take that of John, Thomas or Harry I could never understand. The name or title of her husband gives no additional dignity or character to her, and it sinks her own individuality in him which no woman should allow.

Adam named his wife Eve and we have no account of her ever being called Mrs. Adam. Victoria of England has never called herself Mrs. Albert Saxe-Colburg, nor has Eugenie been known as Mrs. Emperor Louis Napoleon. All married women of any distinction have ever been known by their Christian names. The wife of our first president is known as Martha Washington, instead of Mrs. George Washington.

May the day soon come when women bare honored titles of their own, earned and conferred, but not borrowed.

In the pages of her magazine, Mrs. Bloomer also commented on the opinion of the Tennessee Legislature that, in 1849, had decreed women had no souls and therefore no right to property:

We believe that most women are capable of taking care of their own property, that they have a right to hold it and should dispose of it as they please, man's decision to the contrary not withstanding. As for ourselves, we have no fear but we could take care of a fortune if we had one, without assistance from legislators or lawyers, and we should think them meddling with what did not concern them should they undertake to control it for us.

Ernestine Rose was a Polish Jew who immigrated to the United States in 1838. She became associated with almost every radical movement of the day and horrified even feminine activists because she had no religious affiliation and no belief in the afterlife. In 1851, she spoke these words:

It will be said that the husband provides for the wife or, in other words, he feeds, clothes and shelters her! I wish I could make everyone before me realize the degradation contained in that idea. Yes! He keeps her, and so he does his favorite horse; by law they are both considered his property. Again I shall be told that the law presumes the husband to be kind, affectionate and ready to provide for and protect his wife. But what right, I ask, has the law to entrust the happiness and interest of one being into the hands of another?

A man asked Elizabeth Cady Stanton: *Don't you think that the best thing a woman can do is perform well in the role of wife or mother?* He added: *My wife has presented me with eight beautiful children. Is that not a better life work than exercising the right of suffrage?* Stanton surveyed him from head to foot and answered: *I have met few men worth repeating eight times.*

But there were men who saw the inequity in marriage laws. Matthew Carey in 1830, wrote in his <u>Rules For Husbands and Wives:</u>

Having seen various sets of maxims for the conduct of married life, which have appeared to me to contain very injurious items, degrading to wives, sinking them below the rank they ought to occupy and reducing them to some degree to the level of mere housekeepers and believing them radically erroneous, I annex a set which appear more rational and just than those which I have seen.

1. *A good husband will always regard his wife as his equal; treat her with kindness, respect and attention.*
2. *He will never interfere in her domestic concerns.*
3. *He will always keep her liberally supplied with money for furnishing his table in a style proportioned to his means, and for the purchase of dress suitable to her station in life.*
4. *He will cheerfully and promptly comply with all her reasonable requests, when it can be done, without loss or great inconvenience.*
5. *He will never allow himself to lose his temper toward her by indifferent cookery or irregularity in the hours of meals or any other mismanagement of her servants.*
6. *If she have prudence and good sense, he will consult her on all great operations involving the risk of ruin or serious injury in case of failure. Many a man has been rescued from destruction by the wise council of his wife. Many a foolish husband has most seriously injured himself and*

family by the rejection of the advise of his wife, fearing, lest, if he follow it, he would he regarded as ruled by her!

7. *If distressed or embarrassed in his circumstances, he will communicate his situation to her with candor that she may bear his difficulties in mind of her expenditures.*

When Lucy Stone and Henry Brown Blackwell were married in 1855, they wrote and officially signed a document that they termed a "protest" in the presence of the Reverend Thomas Wentworth Higginson who wrote, in part:

It was with my hearty concurrence . . . that the following protest was read and signed, as part of the nuptial ceremony; and I hope that others may be induced to do likewise.

"PROTEST"

We are acknowledging our mutual affection by publicly assuming the relationship of husband and wife, yet in justice to ourselves and a great principle, we deem it a duty to declare that this act on our part implies no sanction of, nor promise of voluntary obedience to such of the present laws of marriage, as refuse to recognize the wife as an independent, rational being, while they confer on the husband an injurious and unnatural superiority, investing him with legal powers which no honorable man would exercise, and which no man should possess. We protest especially against the laws which give to the husband:

1. *The custody of the wife's person.*
2. *The exclusive control and guardianship of their children.*

3. *The sole ownership of her personal, and use of her real estate, unless previously settled upon her, or placed in the hands of trustees, as in the case of minors, lunatics and idiots.*

4. *The absolute right to the product of her industry.*

5. *Also against laws which give to the widower so much larger and more permanent an interest in the property of his deceased wife, than they give to the widow in that of the deceased husband.*

6. *Finally, against the whole system by which "the legal existence of the wife is suspended during marriage," so that in most States, she neither has a legal part in the choice of her residence, nor can she make a will, nor sue or be sued in her own name, nor inherit property.*

We believe that personal independence and equal human rights can never be forfeited, except for crime; that marriage should be an equal and permanent partnership, and so recognized by law; that until it is so recognized, married partners should provide against the radical injustice of present laws, by every means in their power.

We believe that where domestic difficulties arise, no appeal should be made to legal tribunals under existing laws, but that all difficulties should be submitted to the equitable adjustment of arbitrators mutually chosen.

Thus reverencing law, we enter our protest against rules and customs which are unworthy of the name, since they violate justice, the essence of law.

[signed] Henry B. Blackwell
   Lucy Stone

Perhaps these words of Lucretia Mott sent by Susan B. Anthony to a nephew and his bride on their wedding day will serve as an appropriate codicil to the "protest":

May your independence be equal, your dependence mutual, your obligations reciprocal.

And as early as 1825, Anna Wheeler commented on another aspect of marriage not usually broached by a woman:

She is not permitted to feel or desire . . . . The obedient instrument of man's sexual desire, she is not permitted even to wish for gratification for herself.

Many words, spoken or written by nineteenth century activists, awakened the realization in a growing number of women that marriage stifled their desire for equality. Mary Wollstonecraft, an Englishwoman, was a member of the intellectual circle that included William Godwin and Thomas Paine. One of the first recognized feminists, her book <u>A Vindication of the Rights of Woman</u>, published in 1793, set forth some of the reasons for the inequalities suffered by women. Herewith an example:

Women are told from their infancy and taught by the example of their mothers that a little knowledge of human weakness, justly termed cunning, softness of temper, <u>outward</u> obedience, and a scrupulous attention to a puerile kind of propriety will obtain for them the protection of a man; that they should be beautiful, everything else is needless, for at least twenty years of their lives.

Charlotte Perkins Gilman, having experienced marriage, wrote of her single state in 1882:

This for me to hold to, as I forefear the force of passion should at any time cloud my reason and prevent or benumb my will.

Now that my head is cool and clear, now before I give myself in any sense to another, let me write down my reasons for living single.

In the first place, I am fonder of freedom than anything else. I love to see and be with my friends, but only when I want them. I love to have pleasant faces in my home, but only when I want them.

I like to have my own unaided will in all my surroundings—in dress, diet, hours, behavior, speech and thought.

I <u>increasingly</u> like to feel that my home is <u>mine</u>, that I am free to leave it when I will, and for as long as I will.

I like to select for myself, to provide for myself in every way.

I like to start out in joyous uncertainty of where I am going, and with no force to drive me back—like it beyond words.

I like to go about alone—independently.

The Debris of Centuries

The calculations of James Ussher, (1581-1656) chancellor of St. Patrick's Cathedral in Dublin, later Bishop, then Archbishop of Armagh, became historical truth, dating the existence of the earth to a precise day, month and year: the Creation occurred on the evening of October 22, 4004 B.C. For two centuries this dogmatic calculation, based on the genealogy of the Old Testament, dominated scholarly understanding of the past and was a matter of unquestioning faith and belief. Until the mid-nineteenth century there was little in the study of archaeology to refute long-held beliefs. It was primarily travelers on the "Grand Tour" of Mediterranean Europe and the Middle East who discovered tantalizing evidence of pre-historic sites, bones of animals and humans that clearly led to the existence of a more distant past than that envisioned by Bishop Ussher and succeeding clerics.

In the early decades of the nineteenth century, Americans were caught up in the religious fever of the Second Great Awakening, a Protestant revivalism, fueled by the Reverend Charles Grandison Finney, the greatest American evangelist of the time, who believed every man and woman had to be confronted by the choice between salvation and damnation. A forceful speaker whose voice commanded attention, he preached dramatically, especially addressing young women, converting many with his Calvinistic view of what Almighty God had in store for them.

Troy, New York, was the city where the Reverend Finney had set up shop in the church where many of the Emma Willard Female Academy students attended services. Many years later Elizabeth Cady Stanton described her encounter with the revivalist, perhaps forgetting that she had not been a student at the Academy when Reverend Finney had visited Troy. But great storyteller as she was, her words gave the feeling of terror to those who heard him and fell under his spell. She recalled in her biography written some sixty-five years later:

I can see him now, his great eyes rolling around the congregation and his arms flying about the air like those of a windmill . . . . He described hell and the devil and the long procession of sinners being swept down by the rapids, about to make an awful plunge into the burning depths of liquid fire below . . . . He suddenly halted, and pointing his finger at the supposed procession, he exclaimed: "There, do you not see them?"

I was caught up to such a pitch that I actually jumped up and gazed in the direction to which he pointed while the picture glowed before my eyes and remained with me for months to come.

That experience, imagined or not, encouraged a lifetime of religious skepticism. When Stanton was often reproved for her criticism of the Bible, she said:

To every person who really believes in religious freedom it is no worse to criticize those pages in the Bible that degrade women than it is to criticize those pages in our statute books which degrade her. Everything written by Jew or Greek, Gentile or Christian, by any human being whomsoever, is not too sacred to be criticized by any other human being.

If Elizabeth Cady Stanton should be remembered for but one of her many utterances, this most succinct quotation regarding God and prayer is as relevant today as it was a hundred and fifty years ago:

I distrust those people who know so well what God wants them to do, because I notice it always coincides with their own desires.

Mrs. Stanton also had words to pronounce on the saying of grace:

The usual masculine grace has long been a thorn in my flesh. It is enough to make all the feminine angels weep to see a bumptious man, with a good appetite, spread his hands over a nicely roasted turkey which his little wife has basted and turned two hours in the oven, and thank the Lord as if the whole meal had come down from Heaven, whereas one little pair of hands had like magic produced the whole meal. When I am called on for a grace, here is what I say: Heavenly Father and Mother, make us ever thankful of the patient hands that oft in weariness spread our tables and prepare our daily food. For Humanity's sake. Amen.

Stanton's <u>Woman's Bible</u>, published in 1895, was a commentary on key biblical passages that degraded and subordinated women. It put her at odds with clergy as well as with the majority of her feminist colleagues.

We can make no impression on men who accept the theological view of woman as the author of sin, cursed of God and all that nonsense. The debris of the centuries must be cleared away before our arguments for equality can have the least significance to any of them.

Stanton was worried that most of the woman's movement participants cared more about their religion and the salvation of their souls than about the franchise movement. She "poured out her indignation" in her almost forgotten (even by today's feminists) <u>Woman's Bible</u>.

Theodore Parker, descendent of distinguished Massachusetts forbears, had graduated from Harvard Divinity School. A religious liberal, he rejected Calvinism in favor of free will, stressing individual responsibility for salvation. Parker preached God's presence in each person and His accessibility to men and women. He refused to take scripture literally and suggested that God was an androgynous figure. In his <u>Sermon on the Public Function of Women</u>, delivered in 1853, he said:

If woman had been consulted, it seems to me theology would have been in a vastly better state than it is now. I do not think that any woman would ever have preached the damnation of babies unborn. The popular theology leaves nothing feminine in the character of God. How could it be otherwise, when so much of the popular theology is the work of men who thought woman was a "pollution," and barred her out of all the high places of the church?

If the affairs of the nation had been under woman's joint control, I doubt that we should have butchered the Indians with such exterminating savagery . . . . I doubt we should have spread slavery into nine new states and made it national. I think the Fugitive Slave Bill would never have been an act.

I think man makes a very poor appearance when he says that woman could not do as well as he has done and is doing.

Jonathan Neal was an ardent supporter of women's rights, a committed activist all his life. In 1843, his plea

"Rights of Women" appeared in an editorial in two New York newspapers. He posed this to his readers:

Just reverse the condition of the two sexes—give to women all the power now enjoyed by men . . . . What a clamor there would be then about equal rights, about a privileged class, about being taxed without their consent and all that! And yet, mark my words, that is the true way of putting the question . . . . We have only to ask ourselves how we should bear such laws from women as they are called to bear from us—not only to bear, but to be thankful for? But we are Men—and they are Women; only Women.

But the Reverend John Todd in 1867, continued the age-old comments on the position of women:

The root of the great error of our day is that woman is to be made independent and self-supporting—precisely what she can never be, because God never designed she should be. Her support, her dignity, her beauty, her honor and happiness lie in her dependence as a wife, mother and daughter. Any other theory is rebellion against God's law of the sexes, against marriage which it assails in its fundamental principles and against the family organization, the holiest thing that is left from Eden.

Susan B. Anthony relinquished some aspects of her Quaker upbringing, on occasion attended Unitarian services and made these comments in 1870, regarding personal prayer:

While I do not pray for anybody . . . still I do pray . . . for some terrific shock to startle the women of this nation into a self-respect which will compel them to see the abject degradation of their present condition, which will force them to break their yoke of bondage and give them faith in themselves . . . . The fact is, women are in chains and their servitude is all the more debasing because they do not realize it. O, to compel them to speak and act for their own freedom, though they face the scorn and contempt of the world for doing it.

In 1896, she said:

I pray every second of my life; not on my knees but with my work. My prayer is to lift women to equality with men. Work and worship are one with me.

To a cousin she wrote:

Your little birthday gift, the Book of Proverbs, came duly. Solomon's wise sayings, however, don't help me very much in my work of trying to persuade men to do justice to women. These men for generations back have read Solomon over and over and learned nothing therefrom of fair play for women, and I fear generations to come will continue to read to as little purpose. At any rate, I propose to peg away in accordance with my own sense of wisdom rather than Solomon's. All those old fellows were very good for their time, but their wisdom needs to be newly interpreted in order to apply to people of today.

Harriet Tubman, called the "Moses of her people" led numerous slaves to freedom. She recalled a happening in her earlier years:

I was always praying for poor old master. 'Pears like I didn't do nothing but pray for old master. "Oh, Lord, convert old master; oh, dear Lord, change that man's heart and make him a Christian." And all the time he was bringing men to look at me, and they stood there saying what they would give and what they would take, and all I could say was, "convert old master." Then I heard that as soon as I was able to move I was to be sent with my brothers in the chain gang to the far South. Then I changed my prayer and I said, "Lord, if you ain't never going to change that man's heart, KILL him . . . .

The Women Have Leaped From Their Spheres

The anti-slavery movement of the third decade of the nineteenth century was fueled by Boston journalist William Lloyd Garrison in his newspaper, the Liberator. His view of slavery equated the practices of the South with the racial prejudices of the North and demanded immediate emancipation of all black slaves. In an urgent request to women he specifically cited the position of women slaves, unprotected by the cruelty and lust of men. It was the upper-class women of Boston, primarily of Unitarian and Episcopal denominations, who answered the call and soon formed abolitionist societies. Quaker Lucretia Mott formed the Philadelphia society and a third center of the anti-slavery movement, consisting primarily of Presbyterians, was formed in New York.

Sarah and Angelina Grimké were daughters of a South Carolina slave-holder. They abhorred the institution of slavery, but unable to voice their opinions in the South, they moved to Philadelphia, became Quakers and were soon speaking before anti-slavery groups, giving their first-hand observations. Then, uniting the condition of slaves with the similar condition of women, Sarah Grimké in 1838, spoke these words:

Slave deceives master and master deceives slave; so in marriage relation in thousands of cases. We are told, "The power of woman is in her dependence, flowing from a consciousness of that weakness which God has given her for her protection." If physical weakness is alluded to, I cheerfully concede the superiority; if brute force is what my brethren are claiming, I am willing to let them have all the honor they desire; but if they mean to insinuate that mental or moral weakness belongs more to woman than to man, I utterly disclaim the charge. Our powers of mind have been crushed as far as man could do it, our sense of morality has been impaired by his interpretation of our duties; but nowhere does God say that He made any distinction between us as moral and intelligent beings.

Angelina and Sarah Grimké spoke before mixed or so-called "promiscuous" audiences of men and women, drawing large audiences primarily because they were oddities. Sarah Grimké said:

. . . . Not withstanding what has been urged, woman, I am aware, stands charged to the present day with having brought sin into the world. I shall not repel the charge by any counter assertions, although . . . Adam's ready acquiescence with his wife's proposal does not savor much of that superiority in strength of mind which is arrogated by man. Even admitting that Eve was the greater sinner, it seems to me man might be satisfied with the dominion he has claimed and exercised for nearly six thousand years, and that more true nobility might be manifested by endeavoring to raise the fallen and invigorate the weak, than by keeping women in subjection. But I ask no favors for my sex. I surrender not our claim to equality. All I ask of our brethren is that they take their feet off our necks and permit us to stand upright on that ground which God designed us to occupy.

The lust of dominion was probably the first effect of the fall; and as there was no other intelligent being over whom to exercise it, woman was the first victim of this unhallowed passion . . . . All history attests that man has subjected woman to his will, used her as a means to promote his selfish gratification, to minister to his sensual pleasures, to be instrumental in promoting his comfort; but never has he desired to elevate her to that rank she was created to fill. He has done all he could do to debase and enslave her mind; and now he looks triumphantly on the ruin he has wrought, and says the being he has thus deeply injured is his inferior.

In Sarah Grimké's <u>Letters on the Equality of the Sexes and the Condition of Woman</u>, published in 1838, herewith other examples of contemporary gynephobia:

Woman in all ages and countries has been the scoff and jest of her lordly master. If she attempted to improve her mind, she was ridiculed as pedantic and driven from the temple of science and literature by coarse attacks and vulgar sarcasms. If she yielded to the pressure of circumstances and sought relief from the monotony of existence by resorting to the theatre and the ballroom, by ornamenting her person with flowers and with jewels while her mind was empty and her heart desolate, she was still the mark at which wit and satire and cruelty leveled their arrows.

The early protesters of woman's subservient position were celebrated in Maria Chapman's few lines of ironic, poetic observation written in 1837, the year of Halley's Comet:

Confusion has seized us and all things go wrong.
The women have leaped from their spheres,
And instead of fixed stars, shoot as comets along
And are setting the world by the ears.

In courses erratic they're wheeling through space
In brainless confusion and meaningless chase.

They've taken a notion to speak for themselves
And are wielding the tongue and the pen.
They've mounted the rostrum, the termagant elves.
And, oh horrid, are talking to men . . . .

The world conference of anti-slavery societies met in London in 1840, and proved to be an unexpected awakening of further aspects of the nascent feminist movement. Lucretia Mott and her husband James, along with a goodly number of American men and women, all resolute advocates of abolition, made the eighteen-day voyage. Also on board was Elizabeth Cady Stanton, newly married to abolitionist Henry Stanton. Her father, Judge Cady, had vehemently objected to the marriage, but she was determined to marry the man she loved in a hurried ceremony before they boarded ship. She enlivened the journey by her unladylike activities: calling her husband "Henry" in public, instead of "Mr. Stanton," for persuading the captain to hoist her to the top of the mast in a sailor's sling so she could see far out to sea and for being so unladylike as to beat a distinguished member of the delegation at chess.

The London conference was a deep disappointment to the American women.

They were not to be seated, the men decreed. In fact, with the exception of some of the American men who spoke for their participation, the majority of the gentlemen did not approve of even their presence in the hall.

A compromise was finally voted. The women might be seated in a gallery at the rear of the hall which had been curtained so that they might hear the proceedings but could not see nor be seen. The world-famous abolitionist William Lloyd Garrison was so distressed by the vote that he chose to sit with the women in the curtained gallery and could not be persuaded to give his intended speech.

Mrs. Stanton recalled:

It struck me as very remarkable that abolitionists, who fight so keenly for the slave, should be so oblivious to the equal wrongs of their mothers, wives and sisters . . . . To me there was no question so important as the emancipation of woman from the dogmas of the past.

Lucretia Mott was the first liberal minded woman Mrs. Stanton had ever met and their friendship deepened during the London stay. While walking to their lodgings and commenting on the incidents of the day, they resolved to hold a convention as soon as they returned home and form a society to advocate the rights of women.

However, eight years passed before those plans came to fruition. Mrs. Stanton had filled the intervening years with three energetic boys and was now living in the small town of Seneca Falls, New York, a few miles from the home of Mrs. Mott's sister, Martha Wright, where she was chafing under "mental hunger."

The general discontent I felt with woman's portion of wife, mother, housekeeper, physician and spiritual guide, the chaotic conditions into which everything fell without her constant supervision, and the wearied, anxious look of the majority of women impressed me with a strong feeling that some active measures should be taken to remedy the wrongs of society in general, and of women in particular . . . . It seemed as if all the elements had conspired to impel me to some onward step. I could not see or what to do or where to begin.

Then, on a warm July day in 1848, she received an invitation to tea from Martha Wright, Lucretia Mott's sister. Lucretia and her husband James would also be there. She eagerly accepted and found that in the presence of her mentor from the months in London *"I poured out . . . the torment of my long-accumulating discontent, with such vehemence and indignation that I stirred myself as well as the rest of the party to do and dare anything."* The assembled listeners were inspired to hold a "public meeting for protest and discussion."

Nothing like this had ever been attempted before. They enthusiastically agreed to insert a brief, unsigned notice that very afternoon in the <u>Seneca Falls Courier</u> announcing their woman's rights convention was to take place just four days hence! They obviously felt an urgency but none of them had ever conducted a meeting and only Mrs. Mott had spoken in public before. In making plans for the event, Mrs. Mott cautioned: *"We ought, I think, claim no more for woman than for man; we ought to put woman on a par with man, not invest her with power or call for her superiority over her brother. If we do, she is just as likely to become a tyrant as man is."* The announcement read:

WOMAN'S RIGHTS CONVENTION

A convention to discuss the social, civil and religious condition and rights of Woman will be held at the Wesleyan Chapel, at Seneca Falls, N.Y., on Wednesday and Thursday, the 19th and 20th of July current, commencing at 10 o'clock a.m.

Now they had to devise a statement—a Declaration of Sentiments—similar to the Declaration of Independence. Then, undoubtedly because barely two weeks had passed since the Fourth of July celebration, which brought to mind the overt omission of women from the Declaration, Mrs. Stanton hit upon the solution: "Let us proclaim our own declaration! . . . ."

We hold these truths to be self-evident: that all men and women are created equal . . . . The history of mankind is a history of repeated injuries and usurpations on the part of man toward woman, having in direct object the establishment of an absolute tyranny over her. To prove this, let facts be submitted to a candid world. Then where the colonists had listed the injustices imposed upon them by King George, she paralleled wrongs inflicted upon women by men.

- *He has never permitted her to exercise her inalienable right to the elective franchise.*
- *He has compelled her to submit to laws, in the formation of which she had no voice.*
- *He has made her, if married, in the eye of the law, civilly dead.*
- *He has made her morally an irresponsible being. as she can commit many crimes with impunity, provided they be done in the presence of her husband. In the covenant of marriage, he becoming to all intents and purposes, her master—the law giving him power to deprive her of liberty and to administer chastisement.*

- *He has so framed the laws of divorce, as to what should be the proper causes, and in the case of separation, to whom the guardianship of the children shall be given, as to be wholly regardless of the happiness of women, the law, in all cases, going upon a false supposition of the supremacy of man and giving all power into his hands.*
- *He has denied her the facilities for obtaining a thorough education, all colleges being closed to her.*
- *He has created a false public sentiment by giving to the world a different code of morals for men and women by which moral delinquencies which exclude women from society are not only tolerated, but deemed of little account by men.*

Three hundred women and men came to the little Wesleyan chapel in Seneca Falls for those historic meetings on July 19 and 20, 1848. Most came out of conviction; some out of curiosity; others for the unusual entertainment of seeing women speak in public. On the first day only women were allowed to attend, but on July 20 all were welcome and more than three hundred women and men, many of them Quakers and Congregationalists, filed into the chapel. None of the women felt qualified to chair the proceedings, so James Mott agreed to preside. Elizabeth Cady Stanton delivered her maiden speech:

I should feel exceedingly diffident to speak before you at this time, having never spoken in public, were I not nerved by a sense of right and duty, did I not feel that the time had come for the question of woman's wrongs to be laid before the public, did I not believe that woman herself must do this work; for woman alone can understand the height, the depth, the length and breadth of her degradation.

. . . . We are assembled to protest a form of government existing without the consent of the governed—to declare our right to be free as man is free, to be represented in the government which we are taxed to support, to protest such disgraceful laws as give man the power to chastise and imprison his wife, to take the wages she earns, the property which she inherits and, in the case of separation, the children of her love; laws which make her a mere dependent on his bounty. It is to protest such unjust laws as these that we are assembled today and to have them, if possible, forever erased from our statute books . . . . There can be no true dignity or independence where there is subordination to the absolute will of another, no happiness without freedom.

That afternoon sixty-eight women and thirty-two men signed the document as being in favor of the movement.

Stanton then offered eleven additional resolutions for the convention to vote on. Ten passed easily, but number nine declared it the *duty of the women of this country to secure to themselves their sacred right to the elective franchise.* No one in attendance, not even Lucretia Mott, nor Henry Stanton who hurriedly left town in embarrassment, felt that such a resolution could bring anything but ridicule on the entire proceedings. No woman anywhere on Earth had the right to vote.

Stanton further addressed her audience: . . . . *The right is ours. Have it we must. Use it we will . . . the indomitable wills of many women are already pledged to secure this right . . . .* But these were only brave words and even she feared she would not be able to convince her audience. Her friend Frederick Douglass was present and asked permission to speak.

Although his exact words that afternoon have been lost, his editorial a few days later in his own newspaper, The North Star, stated his position:

All that distinguishes man as an intelligent and accountable being is equally true of woman; and if that government only is just which governs by the free consent of the governed, there can be no reason in the world for denying to woman the exercise of the elective franchise, or a hand in making and administering the laws of the land. Our doctrine is that "right is of no sex."

His words that afternoon helped carry the day. The resolution passed and the convention adjourned.

William Lloyd Garrison in The Liberator approved of the "Woman's Revolution." Horace Greeley in his New York Tribune wrote . . . . *However unwise and mistaken the demand, it is but the assertion of a natural right and as such must be conceded.* The Philadelphia Public Ledger and Daily Transcript editorialized:

Women have enough influence over human affairs without being politicians. Is not everything managed by female influence? Mothers, grandmothers, aunts, sweethearts manage everything. Men have nothing to do but listen and obey . . . .

A woman is nobody. A wife is everything. A pretty girl is equal to ten thousand men and a mother is, next to God, all powerful . . . . The ladies of Philadelphia therefore, under the influence of the most serious, sober second thoughts, are resolved to maintain their rights as Wives, Belles, Virgins and Mothers, and not as Women.

The vast majority of women had no opportunity to be the weak, delicate, charming and graceful beings that men wrote and spoke about. They were household drudges, field hands, mill girls working fourteen hour days, women working to support their families while their husbands drank away their meager wages; and black slavery was still supported by law in one-half the country. Ladies, as such, were far more scarce than men would have their readers believe.

The age of reform was to be! Women's conferences proliferated throughout the northern states. At first women organizers refused to allow any man to speak at their meetings. If one meekly arose to offer a suggestion, he was promptly ruled out of order. What a great satisfaction to do unto them as they had done unto women for centuries. But they soon discovered that to hear from men in meetings made for livelier discussions—both for and against.

Frances Gage was chairwoman at a state convention held in Masselin, Ohio in 1851. As the audience entered the church where the meeting was to be held, a tall black woman walked regally down the aisle and took her seat upon the pulpit steps. She was Sojourner Truth. Mrs. Gage had invited her to be present and to speak if she wished. Mrs. Gage reported: "There ensued a great discussion among the Methodist, Episcopal, Presbyterian and Universalist ministers regarding our resolutions on the rights of women. One claimed superior rights and privileges for man on the ground of 'superior intellect;' another because of the 'manhood of Christ;' if God had desired the equality of woman, He would have given some token of His will though the birth, life and death of the Savior. Another gave his theological view of the 'sin of our first mother.'"

Mrs. Gage continued: "Remember now, there were few women in those days who dared to speak in meeting and the august teachers of the people were seemingly getting the better of us, while the boys in the galleries and the sneerers among the pews were hugely enjoying the discomforture, as they supposed, of the women. Then slowly from her seat in the corner rose Sojourner Truth who, til now, had scarcely lifted her head, She moved slowly and solemnly toward the front, laid her old bonnet at her feet and turned her great speaking eyes to me. There was a great hissing sound of disapprobation above and below. I rose and announced, 'Sojourner Truth' and begged the audience to keep silent for a few moments.

"The tumult subsided at once and every eye was fixed on this almost Amazon form which stood almost six feet high, head erect and eyes piercing the upper air like one in a dream. At her first word there was a profound hush. She spoke in deep tones which, though not very loud, reached every ear in the house and away at the doors and windows."

Well, children, where there's so much racket there must be somethin' out o' kilter. I think that twixt the negroes of the South and the women of the North, all talkin' 'bout rights, the white man will be in a fix pretty soon. But what's all this talkin 'bout?

That man over there say that women needs to be helped into carriages and lifted over ditches and to have the best place everywhere. Nobody ever helps me into carriages or over mud puddles or gives me any best place. And ain't I a woman? Look at me! Look at my arm. I have ploughed and planted and gathered into barns and no man could head me! And ain't I a woman? I could work as much and eat as much as a man—when I could get it—and bear the lash as well! And ain't I a woman? I have borne thirteen children and seen most of them sold off into slavery, and when I cried out with my mother's grief, none but Jesus heard me! And ain't I a woman?

Then they talks 'bout this thing in the head; what that they call it? That's right, honey. Intellect. What's that got to do with women's rights or negroes' rights? If my cup won't hold but a pint and yours holds a quart, wouldn't ye be mean not to let me have my little half measure full?

Then that little man in black there, he say that women can't have as much rights as men 'cause Christ wasn't a woman! Where did your Christ come from? From God and a woman! Man had nothing to do with Him.

If the first woman God ever made was strong enough to turn the world upside down all alone, these women together ought to be able to turn it back and get it right side up again! And now they is askin' to do it, the men better let them. 'Bliged to ye for hearin' on me, and now old Sojourner ain't got nothin' more to say.

Frances Gage reported what ensued: "Amid roars of applause she returned to her seat in the corner, leaving more than one of us with streaming eyes and hearts beating with gratitude. She had taken us up in her strong arms and carried us safely over the slough of difficulty, turning the whole in our favor. I have never seen anything like the magical influence that subdued the mobbish spirit of the day and turned the jeers and sneers of an excited crowd into notes of respect and admiration. Hundreds rushed up to shake her hands and congratulate the glorious old mother and bid her Godspeed on her mission of 'testifyin' again concerning the wickedness of this here people.'"

However, the sin of Eve was not to be silenced, as evidenced by this discourse by an unidentified exhorter:

It was through the seductions of the woman, herself seduced by the serpent, that man fell and brought sin and all our woe into the world. She has all the qualities that fit her to be a helpmeet of man, to be the mother of his children, to be their nurse, their early instructress, their life-long friend; to be his companion, his comforter, his consoler in sorrow, his friend in trouble, his ministering angel in sickness; but as an independent existence, free to follow her own fancies and vague longings, her own ambition and natural love of power, she is out of her element and a social anomaly, sometimes a hideous monster which men seldom are, excepting through a woman's influence. This is no excuse for men, but proves that woman needs a head and restraint of father, husband or priest of God.

While many women bristled at such descriptions and explanations of woman's nature and sphere, still others accepted the restraints imposed upon them and were content to perpetuate their subservient and intellectually demeaning roles. The following is an example of empty-headed foolishness that was read by young women who desired to become socially accepted:

A lady should appear to think well of books, rather than to speak well of them. She may show the engaging light that good taste and sensibility always diffuse over conversation; she may give instances of great and affecting passages because they show the fineness of her imagination or the goodness of her heart; but all criticism beyond this sits awkwardly upon her. She should, by habit, form her mind to the noble and pathetic, and she should have an acquaintance with the fine arts, because they enrich and beautify the imagination; but she should carefully keep them out of view in the shape of learning and let them run through the vein of unpremeditated thought. For this reason she should seldom use and not always appear to understand the terms of art. The gentleman will occasionally explain them to her.

Regardless of such inane twaddle, the reform gauntlet had been thrown down. Young Lucy Stone, speaking extemporaneously at a woman's convention, gave answer to a male speaker who had proclaimed this new movement the product of but a few women, largely those disappointed in marriage or in social status.

The last speaker alluded to this movement as being that of a few disappointed women. From the first years to which my memory stretches I have been a disappointed woman. When with my brothers I reached forth after the sources of knowledge, I was reproved with, "It isn't for you; it doesn't belong to women." Then there was but one college in the world where women were admitted, and that one was in Brazil. I would have found my way there, but by the time I was prepared to go, one was opened in the young state of Ohio—the first in the United States where women and Negroes could enjoy opportunities with white men. I was disappointed when I came to seek a profession worthy of an immortal being—every employment closed to me, except those of teacher, the seamstress and the housekeeper. In education, in marriage, in religion, in everything disappointment is the lot of women. It shall be the business of my life to deepen this disappointment in very woman's heart until she bows down to it no longer . . . .

Leave women to find their sphere. And do not tell us before we are born even that our province is to cook dinners, darn stockings and sew on buttons. We are told woman has all the rights she wants; and even women, I am ashamed to say, tell us so. They mistake the politeness of men for rights—seats while men stand in this hall tonight, and their adulations; but these are mere courtesies. We want rights.

At the Fourth National Woman's conference in 1853, Earnestine Rose parried a male speaker who said it was men who should be held responsible for woman's degraded position. Perhaps to assuage the culpability, Mrs. Rose said she thought women were equally responsible. Gaining the platform, William Lloyd Garrison refuted that notion saying:

. . . . Our eloquent friend, Mrs. Rose, who stood on this platform . . . told us her creed. She told us she did not blame anyone, really, and did not hold any man to be criminal . . . .

For my own part, I am not prepared to respect that philosophy. I believe in sin, therefore in a sinner; in theft, therefore a thief; in slavery, therefore in a slaveholder; in wrong, therefore in a wrongdoer; and unless the men of this nation are made by women to see that they have been guilty of usurpation and cruel usurpation, I believe very little progress will be made. To say all this has been done without thinking, without design, by mere accident, by want of light, can anybody believe this who is familiar with all the facts in this case? There is such a thing as intelligent wickedness, a design on the part of those who have the light to quench it, and to do the wrong to gratify their own propensities, and to further their own interests. So then, I believe that as man has monopolized for generations all the rights which belong to women, it has not been accidental, not through ignorance on his part, but I believe that man has done this through calculation, actuated by a spirit of pride, a desire for domination which has made him degrade woman in her own eyes, and thereby tend to make her a mere vassal.

Lucy Stone, Lucretia Mott, Elizabeth Cady Stanton and men like Wendell Phillips, William Lloyd Garrison and Frederick Douglass participated regularly at state and local conventions. But the woman who was to become the most single-minded advocate of woman's rights didn't convert to the cause until 1851. She was Susan B. Anthony.

Born in 1820, near Adams, Massachusetts, Susan Brownell Anthony was the second daughter of Quaker Daniel Anthony and Lucy Read Anthony, a Baptist, who had given up the singing and dancing she had enjoyed in girlhood when she married. The children were raised in a loving home without ornamentation, without toys, without music or art, adhering to Quaker plainness. Daniel Anthony was a strict temperance man and a staunch friend of Frederick Douglass, a near neighbor. In a time of rampant race prejudice he was an egalitarian and he believed in equal education for girls.

Shortly after Susan was born he started a cotton mill powered by the stream that wound its way through his farm and then staffed it with young women from the surrounding hills. He moved his family to nearby Battenville in 1826, built an impressive fifteen room house and ran several mills, becoming, within a few years, the most important businessman in the area.

Susan attended a district school, but when the male teacher refused to teach her long division, because such lofty knowledge was unnecessary for girls, Daniel started a home school for his children and for the women who worked in his mills. He then hired a series of teachers, one of whom was an independent unmarried woman, trained by Mary Lyon, the educational pioneer. At the age of seventeen Susan was escorted by her father to a Quaker boarding school near Philadelphia where older sister Guelma had already spent a year. The school's curriculum included: "Arithmetic, Algebra, Literature, Chemistry, Philosophy and Bookkeeping"—a far greater array of subjects than those usually taught to girls. Susan spent but one year there. Her father was facing financial ruin; the country was suffering a grim depression. No longer could Daniel Anthony afford tuition for his two daughters. By 1839, all was lost. He was unable to pay notes which came due. All the family's belongings were put on the auction block—everything. Everything belonged to the husband; therefore, everything, even the family's clothes and the household items were destined to be lost.

Susan had been teaching at a district school and, from her meager wages, bought back $11 worth, while Uncle Joshua Read bid for the main part of the household belongings. The family moved to a much smaller house and Susan went to New Rochelle, New York to teach in a Quaker school for girls where she was paid $2 a week. She soon discovered that male teachers were paid $10 weekly. This discrepancy added to her understanding of woman's worth in the marketplace.

At the time of the Seneca Falls Convention Susan was living on her father's farm near Rochester, New York and teaching at a nearby school. She was agitating and speaking for temperance and against slavery and unequal wages for women teachers. She told of her experience at a teachers' convention where the question under debate was: "Why is the profession of teacher less respected than that of doctor, lawyer or minister?" Of the three hundred or so women present none had uttered a single word or had even been invited to comment by the men.

I suddenly rose from my seat in the rear (only men sat up front) and ventured to say, Mr. President! Well, if all the witches that had been drowned, burned or hanged in the Old World and the New had suddenly appeared on the platform, threatening vengeance for their wrongs, the officers of that convention could not have been thrown into greater consternation . . . those frightened men could not decide what to do; how to receive this audacious invader of their sphere of action. The hall went silent. Then the head of the group, an esteemed but arrogant professor from West Point, who was presiding in full dress and gilt buttons, stepped in and asked scornfully, "What will the lady have?" I said, "I wish to speak to the question under discussion." For half an hour the convention debated my request, my right to speak. It was finally granted. This was my first memorable speech:

"It seems to me, gentlemen, that none of you quite comprehend the cause of the disrespect that you complain of. As long as society says a woman has not brains enough to be a doctor, lawyer or minister, but has plenty to be a teacher, every man of you who chooses this profession tacitly admits he has no more brains than a woman. And this, too, is the reason that teaching is a less lucrative profession, as here men must compete with the cheap labor of women. If you would exalt your profession, exalt those who labor with you."

I sat down in the profoundest silence, broken at last by three gentlemen, walking down the aisle to congratulate me on my pluck and perseverance and the pertinency of my remarks. Even the local newspaper wrote: "Whatever the schoolmasters might think of Miss Anthony, it was evident that she hit the nail on the head."

But most of the women were shocked. Some of their comments reached my ears: "I was actually ashamed for my sex;" "I felt so mortified that I really wished the floor would open and swallow me up;" "Who can that creature be? She must be a dreadful woman to get up that way and speak in public;" "I was so mad at those three men making such a parade to shake hands with her. That will just encourage her to speak again."

And she was right. I did speak again and again for equal wages for women teachers, against slavery and race prejudice and for temperance.

Susan soon tired of teaching and spent the next three years organizing women's temperance societies that eventually died for lack of funds, and it became increasingly clear that woman's utter dependence on man for the necessary means to aid reform movements was the great evil. Woman must have a purse of her own and how could this be when the law denies to the wife all right to both individual and joint earnings?

Then, one day in 1851, Amelia Bloomer introduced Susan to Mrs. Stanton on a street corner in Seneca Falls, following a lecture by William Lloyd Garrison. It was a fortuitous beginning to a lifelong friendship. The ensuing decades of work from the impressive triumvirate of Mott, Stanton and Anthony led to the eventual enfranchisement of the majority of our nation's citizens.

In honor of their accomplishments the Portrait Monument of Lucretia Mott, Elizabeth Cady Stanton and Susan B. Anthony was sculpted by well-known artist Adelaide Johnson (1859-1955) in 1920, through a commission from the National Woman's Party. The monument accurately portrays the three suffrage leaders, but the base appears unfinished to convey the suffragists' understanding that winning the right to vote was only the first step toward woman's equality; unfinished to represent the work yet to be done to achieve justice and equality for all.

It was presented as a gift to Congress from the women of the United States in honor of the passage of the Nineteenth Amendment. Although Congress accepted the Portrait Monument in a majestic public ceremony in 1921, it was soon thereafter relegated to the Capitol Crypt. Attempts to move the statue to a place of honor were made in 1928, 1932, 1950, and 1995, but failed. Finally through the efforts of the 104th Congress in 1997, and the Woman's Suffrage Statue Campaign, legislation was passed authorizing the return of the monument to its rightful place in the Capitol Rotunda.

This may be an appropriate time to explain why I have often referred to Susan B. Anthony as "Susan," while conferring the title of "Mrs." to Elizabeth Cady Stanton. During their long friendship Susan always addressed the elder as Mrs. Stanton as did everyone with the exception of Mrs. Mott who familiarly called her "Lizzy." On the other hand, Anthony to friends and associates was "Susan" or "Aunt Susan" by her young associates, her "nieces." "Miss Anthony" was reserved for formal occasions, newspaper accounts or other instances that required propriety.

In the early years of the 1850's, the "Bloomer dress" became the new militant women's rights fashion. It was a Turkish-style costume that Mrs. Stanton's cousin Elizabeth Smith Miller had designed. It gained its name after Amelia Bloomer advocated its use and generally approved of dress reform in the pages of her monthly magazine. The article began: *Although God created us women, He did not command us to wear long petticoats or girt our vital organs.*

The Bloomer dress had a full skirt falling six to eight inches below the knee, full trousers that were gathered at the ankles and, for outdoor use, a Spanish cloak that reached to the knee. Wearing it gave a woman greater freedom whether performing household tasks or attending and speaking at women's rights conventions. But however sensible and practical the costume, wearing it on the street brought forth ridicule from men and disapproval from women who deemed the outfit unladylike.

Soon Elizabeth Cady Stanton, Susan B. Anthony, Lucy Stone, Sarah Grimké and Angelina Grimké Weld were wearing the radical style. The outfit attracted unwelcome attention. During the New York City Woman's Rights Convention of 1853, Anthony and Stone went to mail a letter wearing "the dress." Lucy Stone recalled the experience:

Gradually we noticed we were being encircled. A wall of men and boys gradually shut us in, so that to go on or to go back was impossible. There we stood. The crowd was a good-natured one. They laughed at us. They said impertinent things, and they would not let us out. Every moment brought added numbers who peered over to see what attracted the crowd.

Eventually the women were rescued by the police. Wearing the bloomer costume crossed the boundary between the sexes. Women who wore pants, even those partially covered by a skirt, were trying to be men. Women, it was feared, by appropriating male clothing were also about to demand male privileges, including smoking, military service, voting and governing.

This led to further examples of gynephobia: in 1857, The English Saturday Review headed an article opposing women's rights "Bloomeramia," and a publication in America printed an article in 1855, stating that the Illinois House of Representatives had passed a resolution sardonically stating that "a fine of $100 be hereafter imposed on any lady who shall lecture in public in any part of the state without first putting on gentlemen's apparel." Frances Gage complained in <u>The Lily</u>:

Men cannot get up a picture of a woman's rights meeting . . . but they must put cigars and pipes in our mouths, make us sit cross-legged or hoist our feet above their legitimate positions.

Stanton gave up wearing the bloomer costume in public, but Anthony continued its use enduring the taunts and jeers, the jibes and impertinent remarks for a year and a half, until she realized that the bloomer outfit was becoming a kind of intellectual slavery.

I could never get rid of thinking of myself and the important thing was to forget self. The attention of my audiences was fixed on my clothes instead of my words. Reluctantly I let down my dresses and donned petticoats. To wear any garment that looked like pants claimed the rights of men.

Equal Education = Unequal Remuneration

Today it may seem almost incomprehensible to many that women's brains were considered too small, too weak for learning beyond the mere basics; that her opportunities for employment were restricted to housekeeping and child-rearing; that the few rights she had as a single woman were obliterated upon marriage; that religion held her, as a descendent of Eve, the cause of mankind's sorrows; and that she was to obey the command of the Apostle Paul, who prescribed her silence in church and, by extension, the unseemliness of any woman speaking in public; that society treated woman as a child or somewhat half-witted who had a "proper place" and who must adhere to a strict moral code; that the law denied her the civil, social and political rights enjoyed by men.

In A Vindication of Women's Rights (1792) Mary Wollstonecraft argued that the oppression of middle-class women was largely due to an inadequate education which concentrated on that "weak elegancy of mind, exquisite sensibility and the sweet docility of manners supposed to be the sexual characteristic of the weaker vessel." It was the way they were taught, inhibiting the ability of women to think rationally.

In 1776, Abigail Adams wrote to husband John:

If you complain of neglect of education in sons, what shall I say with regard to daughters, who every day experience the want of it. With regard to the education of my own children I find myself soon out of my depth, and destitute and deficient in every part of education.

A girl's education at that time was generally only rudimentary. Anything beyond the ability to read and write and do simple sums was considered not only unnecessary but a decided drain on female brains. Male medical wisdom decreed that there was a vital connection between the female reproductive system and mental exercises. Any excess mental exertion could cause irreparable damage to the uterus. Knowing too much would lead to neuroses and spinsterhood. A learned woman was an absurdity, an anomaly.

Benjamin Rush in <u>Thoughts Upon Female Education</u> (1787) wrote regarding the necessity of mothers in this new country of the United States to play a vital role in the education of their sons:

The equal share that every citizen has in the liberty and the possible share he may have in the government of our country, make it necessary that our ladies should be qualified in a certain degree, by a particular and suitable education, to concur in instructing their sons in the principles of liberty and government.

The branches of literature most essential for a young lady in this country appear to be:

- *A knowledge of the English language. She should not only read but speak and spell it correctly. And to enable her to do this, she should be taught the English grammar and be frequently examined in applying its rules in common conversation.*

- *Pleasure and interest conspire to make the writing of a fair and legible hand a necessary branch of female education. For this purpose she should be taught not only to shape every letter properly but to pay the strictest regard to points and capitals . . . .*

- *Some knowledge of figures and bookkeeping is absolutely necessary to qualify a young lady for the duties which await her in this country. There are certain occupations in which she may assist her husband with this knowledge and, should she survive him and agreeably to the custom of our country be the executrix of his will, she cannot fail of deriving immense advantages from it.*

- *An acquaintance with geography and some instruction in chronology will enable a young lady to read history, biography and travels with advantage, and, thereby qualify her not only for a general intercourse with the world but to be an agreeable companion for a sensible man. To these branches of knowledge may be added, in some instances, a general acquaintance with the first principles of astronomy and natural philosophy, particularly with such parts of them as are calculated to prevent superstition, by explaining the causes or obviating the effects of nature evil.*

- *Vocal music should never be neglected in the education of a young lady in this country. Besides preparing her to join in that part of the public worship which consists in psalmody, it will enable her to soothe the cares of domestic life. The distress and vexation of a husband, the noise of a nursery, and even the sorrows that will sometimes intrude into her own bosom may all be relieved by song, where sound and sentiment unite to act upon the mind . . . .*

- *Dancing is by no means an improper branch of education for an American lady. It promotes health and renders the figure and motions of the body easy and agreeable. I anticipate the time when the resources of conversation shall be so far multiplied that the amusement of dancing shall be wholly confined to children. But in our present state of society and knowledge, I conceive it to be an agreeable substitute for the ignoble pleasures of drinking and gaming in our assemblies of grown people.*

- *The attention of our young ladies should be directed as soon as they are prepared for it to the reading of history, travels, poetry and moral essays. These studies are accommodated, in a peculiar manner, to the present state of society in America, and when a relish is excited for them in early life, they subdue that passion for reading novels which so generally prevails among the fair sex . . . .*

Some women of wealth established schools for girls in the late eighteenth and early nineteenth centuries: one for respectable young women in Litchfield, Connecticut in 1791, and in Philadelphia, the Young Ladies Academy in 1787. Emma Willard established her Troy Female Seminary in 1814, staunchly believing that young women would make better wives and mothers if they were better educated.

A brochure, depicting the seminary buildings and pleasant surroundings, told of the advantages of Emma Willard's academy in this manner:

This Institution offers the accumulated advantages of nearly fifty years of successful operation. Every facility is provided for a thorough course of useful and ornamental education, under the direction of a corps of more than twenty professors and teachers. The members of the Institution have the benefit of lectures of the highest order on SCIENCE, HISTORY, LITERATURE, ART, &C. &C and the use of a valuable library, an extensive philosophical apparatus, a well-selected cabinet of Minerals and Shells, Maps, Charts and Models. Superior music teachers are constantly employed in the Seminary. Great attention is given to the French language. CLASSES IN DRAWING AND PAINTING, IN OIL AND WATERCOLORS.

Emma Willard's Seminary was the most prestigious school in New York state and this was the school chosen for Elizabeth Cady when she was fifteen and eager to continue her education. She had wanted to attend Union College where her male classmates at Johnstown Academy were going, but no college in America would admit female students. Her father, Judge Cady, thought little of the idea of secondary education for females and wanted his daughter to enjoy "balls and dinners," and to learn "how to keep house and make puddings." It was Elizabeth's brother-in-law who persuaded Judge Cady to allow her to attend Emma Willard's Seminary where she spent three years.

For the vast numbers of girls with no expectations of more than an elementary education, these cynical words written by Sarah Grimké in 1838, applied to them if, indeed, they had any access to her words:

Within the last century it has been gravely asserted that chemistry enough to keep the pot boiling and geography enough to know the location of the different rooms of her house is learning sufficient for a woman.

Immanuel Kant, renowned eighteenth century philosopher, believed that:

Laborious learning or painful pondering, even if a woman should greatly succeed in it, destroys the merits that are proper to her sex.

Many of the male bastions of education were not inclined to change their opinions of female entrance to higher education. In 1869, George Templeton wrote in his diary:

Application from three infatuated young women to Law School: No woman shall degrade herself by practicing law in New York especially, if I can save her. Women's Rights Women are uncommonly loud and offensive of late. I loathe the lot.

When in the 1920's, it was proposed to build a residence hall for women at the University of South Carolina, the editor of the student paper wrote revealing his gynephobic thoughts:

The university will be overrun with girls . . . an effeminate sentimentality will become paramount which is so distasteful to men students . . . . Chapel Hill is a place inherently for men who desire no women around . . . women would only prove a distracting influence, could do no possible good, and would turn the grand old institution into a semi-effeminate college.

But a variety of pro-feminist men expressed, throughout the nineteenth century, their thoughts on the education of girls and women. In 1859, Thomas Wentworth Higginson posed this question:

Ought women to learn the alphabet? There the whole question lies . . . . What sort of philosophy is that which says, "John is a fool; Jane is a genius; nevertheless, John, being a man, shall learn, make laws, make money; Jane being a woman, shall be ignorant, dependent, disfranchised, underpaid . . . ." This formula lies at the bottom of the reasoning one hears every day . . . . Give an equal chance and let genius and industry do the rest. Every man for himself, every woman for herself, and the alphabet for us all.

In Henry Fowle Durant's sermon in September 1877, entitled, "The Spirit of the College," he asks the cooperation of teachers and students "in that revolt which is the real meaning of the Higher Education of Women."

We revolt against the slavery in which women are held by the customs of society—the broken health, the aimless lives, the subordinate position, the helpless dependence, the dishonesties and shams of so-called education. The Higher Education of Women is one of the great world battle-cries for freedom; for right against might. It is the cry of the oppressed slave. It is the assertion of absolute equality.

Education, inevitably, would lead to woman's entrance into the marketplace to compete for jobs held by men. For some employers this was fortuitous because women might work at identical jobs at one-half the pay. In these cases it was argued that man worked to be paid a "family wage," whereas woman worked to pay for her frivolous desires. As early as 1836, the National Trades Union recognized that women were competitors in the labor force and urged employers to increase the pay of men so their wives and daughters would not have to leave their prescribed duties in the home to make ends meet.

In 1852, Horace Greeley wrote:

Society is clearly unjust to woman in according her but four to eight dollars per month for labor equally repugnant with, and more protracted than that of man of equal intelligence and relative efficiency, whose services command from ten to twenty dollars per month. If then, the friends of woman's rights could set the world an example of paying for female service, not the lowest pittance which stern Necessity may compel the defenseless to accept, but as approximately fair and liberal compensation for the work actually done . . . I believe they would give their cause an impulse which could not be permanently resisted.

Virginia Penny summarized the predicament:

A Woman may be defined as a creature that receives half price for all she does, and pays full price for all she needs . . . . She earns as a child—she pays as a man.

Charlotte Woodward attended the first woman's rights convention in 1848, at Seneca Falls and was the only participant still alive in 1920, to cast her first vote. As a young woman she was employed in the glove industry doing piecework in the seclusion of her bedroom. The money she earned was collected and kept by her father. In her memoirs she wrote:

Most women accepted this condition as normal and God-ordained and therefore changeless. But I do not believe there was any community anywhere in which the souls of some women were not beating their wings in rebellion . . . . Every fiber of my being rebelled, although silently, all the hours that I sat and sewed gloves for a miserable pittance which, after it was earned, could never be mine. I wanted to work, but I wanted to choose my task and I wanted to collect my wages.

Even when women entered professional ranks, the moneys due for identical services were usually but one-half. Before the Civil War few women were granted admission to medical colleges. Elizabeth Blackwell would be admitted to the Geneva Medical College in 1847, but only if she were disguised in male clothing. This she refused to do. The male students, upon hearing of her application, thought it a huge joke and thereupon agreed unanimously to admit her. When they learned the school had actually accepted her, they were shocked. After the required two years of study, she became the first female M.D. in the United States.

The Female Medical College of Pennsylvania graduated its first class in 1851. Its founder, Dr. Joseph Longshore, in his valedictory address, warned the new doctors of the many difficulties they would encounter:

Where men and women are engaged in the same vocations, and the labors are equal, and the products of their toil are the same, the compensation of the latter seldom exceeds one-half that of the former. Thus the profits of the employer are doubly enhanced by woman's incessant exertions for an honest and virtuous livelihood.

There was an undercurrent of gynephobia inherent in the words and attitudes of male physicians that seldom was expressed verbally or in written form: the fear that their women patients would prefer women doctors whose fees were less than those of male counterparts. Already in many parts of the country where physicians were few, it was women as nurses and midwives who attended the sick and injured of both sexes and often were more reliable at a birthing.

Often, medical schools reluctantly accepted female students, but made their attendance as uncomfortable as possible with prankish behavior, insults, taunts, snide remarks. Lucy Wanzer entered medical school in California in 1872, where not only students but professors engaged in insulting behavior. She had petitioned the Board of Regents for admission to the college. Thus ordered to accept her as a student, the dean decided to make her life miserable by distributing the following to the male students:

We have to accept this female student, as she has the best of us. The law has been decided in her favor, but you can make it so uncomfortable that she cannot stay. We will get rid of her in short order. Of course she will complain, but we will say that we are very sorry but we cannot lecture to two classes. With just one woman we will make short work of it.

In his address "Upon the Opening of the Johns Hopkins Medical School to Women" in 1881, James Cardinal Gibbons said:

The attendance of female physicians upon women is often of incalculable benefit. Much serious and continued suffering is undergone by women, and many beginnings of grave illnesses are neglected, because of the sense of delicacy which prevents them from submitting to the professional services of men. There is also an infinite number of cases, known to all who have been concerned in charitable or reformatory work, in which no influence or assistance can be so effectual as that of a physician who is also a woman . . . .

Prominent English woman's rights advocate Josephine Butler commented after consulting a woman doctor:

I must say that I gained more from her than from any other doctor . . . because I was able to tell her so much more than I ever could or would tell to any man. O, if only men knew what women have to endure, and how every good woman has prayed for the coming of this.

Aleta Jacobs, the first female doctor in the Netherlands, speaking of poor women said:

From these women I learnt that they suffered a great deal from too many and too frequent pregnancies, but careful inquiry convinced me that if I could advise nothing but sexual abstinence as a means of avoiding pregnancy, my advise would be useless for, in the conditions under which they lived, abstinence was impracticable.

In an address before the Association of College Teachers in 1886, Melvil Dewey approved the hiring of female college graduates as librarians. He promoted the profession for college-bred women where their salaries could equal that of men in the same field.

There is almost nothing in the higher branches which she cannot do quite as well as a man of equal training and experience; and in much of library work woman's quick mind and deft fingers do many things with a neatness and dispatch seldom equaled by her brothers.

Experience has taught me why the fairest employers, in simple justice, usually pay men more for what seems at first sight the same work.

Mr. Dewey then rationalized the lower pay accorded to women librarians in four numbered paragraphs. These reasons might explain the wage inequities in other professions as well.

1. *Women have usually poorer health and as a result lose more time from illness and are crippled by physical weakness when on duty. The difficulty is most common*

to women, as are bright ribbons and thin shoes and long hair, but it is a question of health, not of sex. A strong healthy woman is worth more than a feeble man for the same reason that a strong man gets more than a weak woman.

2. Usually women lack business and executive training. Her brothers have been about the shops and stores and in the streets or on the farm hearing business matters transacted from earliest childhood. The boys have been trading jack knives and developing the business bumps while the girls are absorbed with their dolls. It would be a miracle at present if girls were not greatly inferior in this respect and it is this fact which accounts for so few prominent chief librarianships being held by women. But this is the fault of circumstances, not necessarily of sex, and women who have somehow got the business ideas and training and have executive force are getting the salaries that such work commands. When girls have as good a chance to learn these things, I doubt not that they will equal their brothers and will keep cash and bank accounts and double entry books for their private affairs. A man brought up girl-fashion, as not a few are, proves just as helpless on trial and as a result gets only a "woman's salary."

3. Lack of permanence in her plans is one of the gravest difficulties with women. A young man who enters library work and later thinks of a home of his own, is stimulated to fresh endeavors to make his services more valuable. Many a young man's success in life dates from the new earnestness which took possession of him on his engagement. But with women the probability or even the possibility that her position is only temporary and that she

will soon leave it for home life does more than anything else to keep her value down. Neither man nor woman can do the best work except when it is felt to be the life work. This lack of permanence in the plans of women is more serious than you are apt to realize. If woman wishes to be as valuable as a man, she must contrive to feel that she has chosen a profession for life and work accordingly. Then she will do the best that is in her to do as long as she is in the service, and if at any time it seems best to change her state, the work already done has not been crippled by this "temporary" evil.

4. *With equal health, business training and permanence of plans, women will still usually have to accept something less than men because of the consideration which she exacts and deserves on account of her sex. If a man can do all the other work just as well as the woman and in addition can in an emergency lift a heavy case, or climb a ladder to the roof or in case of accident or disorder can act as fireman or do police duty, he adds something to his direct value just as a saddle horse that is safe in harness and not afraid of the cars will bring more in nine markets out of ten than the equally good horse that can be used only in the saddle. So in justice to those who wish to be fair to women, remember that she almost always receives, whether she exacts it or not, much more waiting on and minor assistance than a man in the same place and therefore, with sentiment aside, hard business judgment cannot award her quite as much salary. There are many uses for which a stout corduroy is worth more than the finest silk.*

One might wonder how well the assembled college graduates, among them many women, were assuaged by his words concerning unequal wages. Certainly in the present century, readers, be they male or female, would find Mr. Dewey's arguments more than ridiculous. Hence, it has been my pleasure to repeat them!

Myra Bradwell graduated from law school but was rejected from the bar because she was a woman. However, she put her training in the law to use by publishing the Chicago Legal. In connection with her failure to practice her chosen profession the United States Supreme Court issued this edict in 1868:

The natural and proper timidity and delicacy which belongs to the female sex evidently unfits it for many occupations of civil life . . . . The paramount destiny and mission of women are to fulfill the noble and benign office of wife and mother. This is the law of the Creator.

Arabella Mansfield was the first woman admitted to the bar in the United States in 1869. However, she did not practice law, but became a university professor.

Charlotte Ray was the first black woman admitted to the bar. She had graduated Phi Beta Kappa from Howard University Law School and then opened an office in Washington, D.C. in 1872.

William T. Harris in 1901, argued the place for women in law by giving his reasons "Why Many Women Should Study Law:"

Here I base my argument on behalf of the necessity not only for an increase of law students in general, but especially of women students of law. I have heard it asked whether the profession is not overstocked? Are there not more lawyers than can make a living at their profession? I answer by calling attention to the increase of great business combinations and to the utter necessity of professionally skilled legal advice in every new issue. We need greater specialization and more expert skill on the part of the legal council. Here is woman's opportunity. She will not be so much required as lawyer in criminal cases as lawyer in civil cases; she will not be required so much in actual control of civil cases in the courts, as in the office giving professional advice in advance, giving advice which will prevent law suits, rather than skillfully extricating the client who has been so unfortunate as to be brought into court. This, in my thinking, is a much more noble view of the profession of law. I hold that the lawyer of the future is to find his or her chief function in preventing law suits.

. . . The natural characteristic of the feminine temperament is not favorable to the legal consideration of a subject. Sentiment and impulse predominate those rather than a cold investigation of the forms of justice which protect society as a whole. An interest in legal studies is less likely to be a feminine than a masculine trait. By all means, therefore, one would say that the study of law is desirable on the part of many women. It has often been remarked by wise philosophers in politics that the United States succeeds in the experiment of self-government especially through the services of its lawyers. For the lawyers abound not only in the courts of justice but in the legislative chambers. The lawyer serves his country not only in helping interpreting the law in the court but also in the legislature in making a law that does not contradict itself or subvert the fundamental law of the state.

I will add an element of strength to the mind of woman to acquire the judicial way of looking at human deeds and actions—to acquire what is known as a "legal mind." And it will not be at the expense of the high traits of character which are recognized as feminine.

I therefore predict great success and great influence ultimately from this movement which brings woman into the professions and especially into the profession of law.

Perhaps the exploits of Belva Lockwood (1830-1917) had escaped the memory of Mr. Harris when he penned his words noting the limits of female lawyers. Perhaps she had already been written out of history despite her many accomplishments. Belva Lockwood was determined to study law, even though denied admittance to the Columbian Law School in the District of Columbia whose trustees feared she would be a distraction to male students. Accepted in 1870, to the new National University Law School, along with several other women, she was denied a diploma on completion of her studies in 1873, because she was a woman. She then wrote a letter to President Ulysses S. Grant stating she had passed all her courses and deserved a diploma. Within a week after posting the letter, Lockwood received her degree at age 43. She was admitted to the D.C. bar although several judges were outspoken in their lack of confidence in her. Trying to gain admittance to the bar in Maryland, she was lectured by a judge who told her that God Himself had determined that women were not equal to men and never would be. The judge suppressed her attempts to answer by saying she had no right to speak. He then had her removed from the courtroom.

She lobbied Congress from 1874 to 1879 to pass an anti-discrimination bill allowing women lawyers the same access to the bar as men. Finally passed by Congress, it was signed into law by President Rutherford B. Hayes. Belva Lockwood became the first woman member of the U.S.

Supreme Court bar on March 3,1879, and late in 1880, she became the first woman lawyer to argue a case before the U.S. Supreme Court.

Representing the National Equal Rights party Lockwood ran in the presidential elections of 1884 and 1888, the first woman to make a serious bid for the presidency. (Victoria Woodhull had attempted a similar bid in 1872, but among other difficulties, she was of insufficient age to seek the presidency.) It was estimated that Belva Lockwood received some 4,000 votes in 1884. It was certainly unusual that she received any votes. Women could not vote and newspapers referred to her as "old lady Lockwood" and warned men of the danger of "petticoat rule." Lockwood, not to let an opportunity lapse, petitioned Congress to have her votes counted. She asserted via newspapers and magazines that she had evidence of voter fraud: supporters' ballots had been ripped up, she had "received one-half the electoral vote in Oregon, and votes in Pennsylvania had been simply dumped in a waste basket."

Her two presidential bids gained her the fame needed for her lecture appearances promoting woman suffrage and world-wide human rights.

Wipe the Dew Off Your Spectacles

Elizabeth Cady Stanton spoke extensively and wrote prodigiously regarding women's lack of equality in domestic, social and political areas or based on religious precepts.

From "Man Cannot Speak For Her" 1849:

But what would a woman gain by voting? Men must know the advantages of voting for they all seem very tenacious about the right, Think you, if woman had a voice in the government, that all those laws affecting her interests would so entirely violate every principle of right and justice? Had woman a vote to give, might not the office-holders and seekers propose some change in her condition?

"But are you not already represented by your fathers, husbands. brothers and sons?" Let your statute books answer the question. We have had enough of such representation. In nothing is woman's true happiness consulted. Men like to call her an angel—to feed her what they think is sweet food—nourishing her vanity, to make her believe that her organization is so much finer than theirs, that she is not fitted to struggle with the tempests of public life but needs their care and protection!! Care and protection—such as the wolf gives the lamb—such as the eagle the hare he carries to his eyrie!! Most cunningly he traps her and then takes from her all those rights which are dearer to him than

life itself—rights which have been baptized in blood and the maintenance of which even now is rocking to their foundations the kingdoms of the Old World . . . .

And in an address to the New York Legislature, 1854, she said:

Would to God you could know the burning indignation that fills a woman's soul when she turns over the pages of your statute books and sees there how like feudal barons you free men hold your women. Would that you could know the humiliation she feels for her sex when she thinks of all the beardless boys in your law offices, learning these ideas of one-sided justice, taking their first lessons in contempt for all womankind, being indoctrinated into the incapacities of their mothers and the lordly absolute rights of man over woman, children and property.

Then in another address to the New York Legislature in 1860:

. . . . There is a kind of nervous unrest always manifested by those in power whenever new claims are started by those out of their own immediate class. The philosophy of this is very plain. They imagine that if the rights of this new class be granted, they must, of necessity, sacrifice something of what they already possess. They cannot divest themselves of the idea that rights are very much like land, stocks, bonds and mortgages and that, if every new claimant be satisfied, the supply of human rights must in time run low. You might as well carp at the birth of every child, lest there should not be enough air left to inflate your lungs, at the success of every scholar for fear that your draughts at the fountain of knowledge could not be so long and deep, at the glory of every hero, lest there be no glory left for you.

In answer to one of Stanton's speeches before the New York Legislature regarding an amendment to the existing property law which provided that women should not only control whatever property they inherited but could also own and control whatever money they earned, an august senator speculated with self-serving humor:

Women always have the best seats in the cars, carriages and sleighs, the warmest place in the winter and the coolest place in the summer. They have their choice on which side of the bed they will lie, front or back. And therefore, if there is any inequality or oppression in the case, the gentlemen are the sufferers. On the whole, the Committee have concluded to recommend no measure, except that as they have observed several instances in which husband and wife have both signed the petition. In such case they would recommend the parties to apply for a law authorizing them to change clothing, so that the husband may wear petticoats and the wife the breeches, and thus indicate to their neighbors and the public the true relation in which they stand to each other.

The whole house erupted into roars of laughter.

Two one-line quotes of Mrs. Stanton reveal not only the succinctness of her words but of their appropriateness:

- *Come, come, my conservative friend, wipe the dew off your spectacles and see that the world is moving.*
- *Men have so long exercised political power in the world that they have come to look upon it as a masculine attribute, like the beard.*

When the Civil War broke out in 1861, it all but put an end to the agitation for woman's rights. Lucy Stone, Stanton and Anthony organized the National Woman's Loyal League and lobbied for the passage of the Thirteenth Amendment which would abolish slavery. Over 400,000 signatures were collected on petition to send to Congress. The Thirteenth Amendment was passed by Congress and ratified by the states. But to ensure the rights of the newly freed slaves, the Fourteenth Amendment was proposed to give them the rights of citizenship, including the right to vote. It was important that this amendment apply to women as well. That was not to be. The amendment specifically defined voters as male; the first time the word "male" had penetrated the Constitution.

The Fifteenth Amendment was proposed when some states tried to deprive the black man of the franchise. It read: "The right of citizens of the United States to vote shall not be denied or abridged by the United States or by any state on account of race, color or previous condition of servitude."

Though some women saw an opportunity to use the wording of the new amendment to test their ability to gain the long desired vote, it was Susan B. Anthony's vote in the 1872 election that gained the most notoriety. She had consulted Judge Henry Seldon in this regard and it was his opinion that the odds were in her favor. Therefore, two days before the election, she and two of her sisters presented themselves before the election officials at a polling place near their home in Rochester, New York. The inspectors were dumfounded to see them, but Anthony finally convinced them that the Constitution gave them the citizen's right to the franchise. They were allowed to register and two days later they voted!

Three weeks later, the Deputy Marshall of Rochester arrested Anthony at her home. She instructed the deputy to wait while she changed into what she termed "more appropriate dress" and then extended her hands to await the requisite handcuffs. The embarrassed deputy demurred. When they arrived at the courthouse she was surprised to find that the inspectors had been arrested as had the fourteen other women from her ward who had voted. All had been released on bail, but Anthony applied for a writ of *habeas corpus* which was promptly denied and her bail was doubled. Not intending to pay one dollar of bail money, she was prepared to go to jail. Instead Judge Selden insisted on paying her bail, thereby renouncing her right to bring the case to a higher court. Seldon had conceded to chivalry: "I could not see a lady I respected put in jail." Now, being at liberty until her trial, Anthony set out to speak in as many post office districts of Monroe County as possible.

The following was written by a young reporter as he covered her speaking throughout the county:

. . . . *Certain erring "sisters" voted at the November election. For this they were arrested and indicted. The venue was laid in Monroe County and there the trial was to take place. Miss Anthony then proceeded to stump Monroe County and every town and village thereof, asking her bucolic listeners . . . "Is it a crime for a United States citizen to vote?" The answer generally is in the negative and so convincing is Sister Anthony's rhetoric that it is supposed that no jury can be found to convict her. The district attorney has, therefore, postponed the trial and changed the place thereof to Ontario County; whereupon the brave Susan takes the stump in Ontario . . . . It is a regular St. Anthony's dance she leads the district attorney; and in spite of winter cold or summer heat, she will carry her case from county to county as fast as the venue is changed.*

The trial was held in Ontario County in June of 1873. Justice Ward Hunt presided, listening to the arguments of

Susan's lawyer, Henry Selden, and to those of the opposition, and he immediately submitted a written opinion that the Fourteenth and Fifteenth Amendments could not be construed as giving women the right to vote. He then instructed the jury to render a guilty verdict. When Mr. Seldon objected and demanded the jury be polled, the judge dismissed the jury.

The judge then asked if the prisoner had anything to say why sentence should not be passed.

Yes, Your Honor, I have many things to say, for in your ordered verdict of guilty, you have trampled underfoot every vital principle of our government. My natural rights, my political rights, my civil rights, my judicial rights are all alike ignored. Robbed of the fundamental privilege of citizenship, I am degraded from the status of citizen to that of a subject. And not only myself individually, but all of my sex are by Your Honor's verdict doomed to political subjection . . . .

The judge said: "The Court cannot listen to a rehearsal of arguments that the prisoner's council has already consumed three hours in presenting."

But your Honor will not deny me this one and only poor privilege of protest against this high-handed outrage upon my citizen's rights. May it please the Court to remember that since the day of my arrest last November, this is the first time that either myself or any person of my disfranchised class has been allowed a word of defense before judge or jury.

All my prosecutors, from the 8th Ward corner grocery politician who entered the complaint to the United States Marshall, Commissioner, District Attorney, District Judge, Your Honor on the bench, not one is my peer. But each and all are my political sovereigns; and had Your Honor submitted my case to the jury, as was clearly your duty, even then I should have just cause for protest, for not one of those men was my peer; but native or foreign born, white or black, rich or poor, awake or asleep, sober or drunk, each and every man of them was my political superior, in no way my peer.

The judge then insisted I had been tried according to the established forms of law.

Yes, Your Honor, but by forms of law all made by men, interpreted by men, administered by men, in favor of men and against women.

When I was brought before Your Honor for trial, I hoped for a broad and liberal interpretation of the Constitution and its recent Amendments that should declare all United States citizens under its protective aegis—that should declare equality of rights the national guarantee to all persons born or naturalized in the United States. But failing to get this justice, failing even to get a trial <u>not</u> of my peers, I ask not leniency at your hand—but rather the full rigors of the law.

"The Court must insist," Judge Hunt began. *At this point I sat down.* The judge continued, "The prisoner will stand up." *I rose.* "The sentence of the Court is that you pay a fine of one hundred dollars and the costs of the prosecution."

May it please Your Honor, I shall never pay a dollar of your unjust penalty. All the stock in trade I possess is a $10,000 debt, incurred by publishing my newspaper—<u>The Revolution</u>—four years ago, the sole object of which was to educate all women to do precisely as I have done: rebel against your man-made, unjust, unconstitutional forms of law that tax, fine, imprison and hang women, while they deny them the right of representation in the government; and I shall work on with might and main to pay *very dollar of that honest debt, but not a penny shall go to this unjust claim.*

She never did pay that fine. It was neither pardoned nor remitted. There is evidence, however, that Henry Seldon paid her fine just as he had paid her bail.

A grand celebration was planned for the American Centenary on July 4, 1876, in Philadelphia where the Declaration of Independence had been signed. It was also the site of the Centennial Exhibition. Some women suffrage members, finding little to celebrate, had planned to drape themselves in black and carry placards reading: TAXATION WITHOUT REPRESENTATION IS TYRANNY. They decided instead to make themselves known in a more intrusive manner. Since Anthony was the only single woman among them and, therefore, the only one able to enter into a business contract, (the other women would need their husband's signature) she rented rooms near Independence Hall.

Now Anthony and Stanton, with their colleague Matilda Joslyn Gage, had to write a new Declaration of Rights for Women. Different from the Declaration written almost thirty years before at the first woman's convention, it no longer needed to deal with equal education, the right to earn a living, to speak in public. It was not just men who were the oppressors but rather the government that "deserved to be impeached" for keeping women from enjoying "the broad principles of human rights" proclaimed in 1776. "We protest against this government of the United States as an oligarchy of sex and not a true republic; and we protest against calling this a centennial celebration of the independence of the United States."

Their next job was to get the Declaration onto the program of the official Fourth of July ceremony. Stanton wrote to General Hawley of Connecticut, president of the Centennial Commission, requesting fifty seats for the officers of the National Woman's Suffrage Association (NWSA) but he refused, saying there was no room, even for his wife. Stanton then asked permission to present the Declaration to the President of the United States "as an historical part of the proceedings." The general said it was too late. All arrangements had been made and programs printed. Stanton told him that "men had run this government for a hundred years without consulting the women of the United States." The answer was still no and Hawley added: "We propose to celebrate what we have done the last hundred years, not what we have failed to do."

Anthony had obtained a press pass for herself through her brother's Kansas newspaper. Hawley then managed to find four more seats. Stanton and Lucretia Mott refused them, now considering them an insult. Anthony gave the tickets to four co-workers. The afternoon was filled with patriotic speechmaking. When the descendent of one of the signers of the Declaration of Independence finished the reading, the fortunate four, led by Anthony, began making their way to the podium. Stunned to see Anthony approaching, the acting vice-president, Michigan Senator Thomas W. Ferry, accepted with a low bow the rolled-up parchment copy of the Woman's Declaration. Anthony turned and walked back up the aisle, her friends handing out copies of the Declaration to whomever reached for one. There was a good deal of excitement as men climbed over seats in their enthusiasm and General Hawley banged his gavel and shouted for order again and again.

Once outside in Independence Square, Anthony commandeered a bandstand set up for that night's patriotic concert. She spoke to the crowd gathered to hear her read the Declaration of Rights for Woman:

Woman has shown equal devotion with man to the cause of freedom and has stood firmly at his side in its defense. And now, at the close of a hundred years, as the hour-hand of the great clock that marks the centuries points to 1876, we declare our faith in the principle of self-government, our full equality with man in natural rights; that woman was made first for her own happiness, with the absolute right to herself—to all the opportunities and advantages life affords for her complete development; and we deny the dogma of the centuries, incorporate in the codes of all nations—that woman was made for man—her best interests—to be sacrificed to his will. We ask our rulers that all civil and political rights that belong to the citizens of the United States be guaranteed to us and to our daughters forever.

Daniel Livermore, husband of suffragist Mary Livermore, wrote "Woman Suffrage Defended" in 1885:

Notwithstanding our democratic theories and our Fourth of July "orations," which are largely "glittering generalities," our government is not a true democracy. In no proper sense do "the people" govern, and hence we practically deny the fundamental principles upon which our government is based—the government of the people, when in fact, the few govern the many . . . .

This startling fact not only arrests our attention, but shows the fallacy of our democratic pretensions, that this is a government of the people and by the people! Women are "people," and are as much entitled to the ballot as men, but they are defrauded by men of that right or privilege, and are unjustly excluded from all participation in the administration of government.

When men assume the right to make laws for women to obey under penalty of fine, imprisonment or death, it is not merely a "stinging insult" to woman, it is the cruelest kind of despotism and subjugation, which men would not submit to for a moment!

One western territory of the United States gained suffrage for its women in 1869. Its story bares telling. At that time South Pass City, a mining town of 3,000 inhabitants, was the largest city in the Territory of Wyoming. Mrs. Esther Morris, the wife of a miner, had been elected the local Justice of the Peace, the first woman anywhere in the world to hold that position. A few days before the first territorial election, she held a tea party to which she invited twenty of the most influential citizens of the town, including the two candidates running for the Territorial Legislature. Mrs. Morris elicited from each candidate a promise to introduce a bill in the new legislature that would give the vote to women. The Democratic candidate Col. William Bright said he would and the Republican Herman Nickerson agreed as well.

Col. Bright won the election and introduced the woman suffrage bill a few days after the legislative session began. The legislature was composed entirely of Democrats, but the governor was a Republican, holding the power of veto. The Senate passed the bill. When it was introduced in the House, one group set out to kill it with amendments, such as the age requirement for female voters be set at thirty years, for no woman, theorized the men, would admit to being that age. The bill finally passed the House and was now in Governor

John Campbell's hands. Many of the men who had voted for it were certain the Republican governor would veto it.

But there was something in Campbell's background that the legislators knew nothing of. As a young man he had lived in Salem, Ohio, one of the early woman's suffrage sites and had been so interested in oratory that he had attended the convention expressly to hear Susan B. Anthony speak. Her words had convinced him to favor woman suffrage. He signed the bill on December 10, 1869, and for the first time in the history of the world women had won the legal right to vote.

Twenty years later in 1889, when Wyoming Territory applied for statehood, the suffrage article of the territory's constitution came under attack in the U.S. House of Representatives. Rumors were strong that Wyoming would not be admitted to the Union unless the suffrage law was abolished. A group of Cheyenne women telegraphed the territory's delegate in Washington saying:

DROP US IF YOU MUST. WE CAN TRUST THE MEN OF WYOMING TO ENFRANCHISE US AFTER OUR TERRITORY BECOMES A STATE.
But the Wyoming Legislature had also telegraphed the delegate:
WE MAY STAY OUT OF THE UNION A HUNDRED YEARS, BUT WE WILL COME IN WITH OUR WOMEN.

Wyoming's bill of admission to statehood was passed into law by the narrow margin of 133 to 127 in the House and 29 to18 in the Senate.

By the end of the nineteenth century, despite the urgings of many more men who saw the unfairness, the injustice of denying the vote to women, only three more states entered the roll of woman suffrage: Colorado, Utah and Idaho.

Colorado was the first state to win suffrage at a general election. In 1893, Denver was a major urban center with some important industry and a somewhat shaky moral reputation.

The Territory of Utah adopted equal suffrage in 1890, mainly to preserve dominance over a growing Gentile minority consisting mainly of men. In 1896, now seeking statehood, church leaders encouraged women to take defense of polygamy by demanding their rights as women to choose their own marriage style. But Utah became a state only when polygamy was no longer a choice.

Idaho was admitted to the Union in 1896. The largely male population felt female suffrage might encourage more women to make the westward trek.

Not until 1910, did another state grant voting rights to women. That was Washington. California enfranchised women in 1911, succeeding by only 3,587 votes, an average of but <u>one</u> vote in each precinct in the state. Oregon, Kansas and Arizona adopted suffrage in 1912; Illinois in 1913; Montana and Nevada in 1914; New York in 1917; Michigan, South Dakota and Oklahoma in 1918. By 1914, all the western states, with the exception of New Mexico, had granted suffrage to women. Six years later the New Mexico Legislature was to experience a down-to-the-wire ratification before the final day of its meeting.

It was, in large part, the liquor lobbyists in most states who persuaded voters to deny woman suffrage. Wisconsin fearfully distributed leaflets such as this one:

DANGER!
Woman's Suffrage Would Double
The Irresponsible vote
A Menace to the Home, Men's
Employment and to All Business

The New, Enlightened, Fearless Eve

In the last few years of the nineteenth century as feminism expanded with more college educated and working women entering the ranks, there was a concentrated effort by clergy of various denominations to curb the growing demand for woman's equality. The myth of Eve as a temptress, sinner, despoiler of God's intended perfection for humankind was exploited with a vengeance. But feminists asserted that Eve now had a new role, distinctly different from the male Biblical understanding. Formerly, Eve and all subsequent females were destined to occupy second-class status, saved only by religion and childbearing. Now, the new Eve would be elevated to the position of a seeker of knowledge as women found new meaning in the Adam versus Eve account.

It was Elizabeth Cady Stanton, a convert to the Freethinker movement in the 1880's, who would change the well-worn Garden of Eden story in her Woman's Bible. Freethinkers, focused on replacing religious superstition with a belief in rational, scientific thought, believed the Bible and its priestly interpreters contributed to the degraded condition of women.

In 1886, Stanton wrote:

It is humiliating for a woman of my years to stand up before men twenty years younger and ask them for the privilege of enjoying my rights as a citizen in a republic . . . . We can make no impression on men who accept the theological view of woman as the author of sin, cursed by God and all that nonsense.

Adding to the obstacles of woman's equality, Stanton believed the clergy corrupted the liberal teachings of Jesus. In 1885, she wrote:

I have passed from the political to the religious phase of this question, for I now see more clearly than ever, that the arch enemy to woman's freedom skulks behind the altar.

Then, perhaps recalling the harrowing words of Charles Grandison Finney and her subsequent failed conversion, she wrote:

No class of men should have such power to pervert the religious sentiments and oppress mankind with gloomy superstitions through life and an undefined dread of the unknown after death.

To liberate women from a misogynist religion, replacing it with the assertion of individual conscience, based on science and reason, the Bible "rightly interpreted" would become Stanton's final challenge. In 1886, she wrote in a letter to a friend:

If we could get twenty-five intelligent, well-educated good common sense women, we could make "The Woman's Bible" a great feature of the general uprising in this nineteenth century.

Stanton's serious work on the Bible project for the next nine years was sporadic, often languid, due to difficulties in procuring women writers who felt as interested in her enterprise as she did. Each member of the <u>Woman's Bible</u> committee would have her commentaries on a particular book of the Bible published in the <u>Woman's Tribune</u>, a liberal suffrage paper. The final version of the <u>Woman's Bible</u> would then be settled by committee and published in book form. The commentary on Genesis, consisting of fifty-four pages, was the most extensive, refuting the clerical held belief of the "sin" of Eve. Now, rather than considering Eve in terms of her sin and subsequent punishment, her actions in the Garden of Eden indicated a higher, nobler motivation for her behavior. Eve had "fallen" as a result of woman's "natural" instinct for knowledge. A male commentator made this observation:

The unprejudiced reader must be impressed with the courage, the dignity, and the lofty ambition of the woman. The tempter evidently had found a profound knowledge of human nature and saw at a glance the high character of the person . . . . Compared with Adam she appears to great advantage through the entire drama.

However, most clergymen warned that an unbridled thirst for knowledge would lead to the destruction of society, for knowledge without religion *does but increase a power . . . which may be ruinous . . . though knowledge be power, yet it is not virtue.*

Lillie Devereux Blake, a contributor to the revised Genesis, wrote in regard to Adam's behavior:

The subsequent conduct of Adam was to the last degree dastardly . . . . When his sin is discovered by God . . . . Adam endeavors to shield himself behind the gentle being he has declared to be so dear. "The woman thou gavest to be with me, she gave me and I did eat," he whines—trying to shield himself at his wife's expense! To Blake's amazement *that upon such a story men have built up a theory of their superiority.*

The <u>Woman's Bible</u> collaborators felt the need to rescue the Garden of Eden drama, rather than have science declare it false. Stanton, perhaps to placate the overwhelming number of women who steadfastly believed the Biblical account, wrote:

We are equally pleased with her attitude, whether as myth in an allegory or as the heroine of an historical occurrence.

The <u>Woman's Bible</u> was soundly denounced by suffrage leaders, staunchly believing the project was not only ill-conceived, but that it was hurting the cause for equality, especially in the South. This final work of Elizabeth Cady Stanton proved a catastrophe for her reputation. Younger suffragists concentrated on the path to enfranchisement and civil equality, not to be undermined by religious questions and arguments.

In the early days of the twentieth century of one thing the suffragists could be certain and Stanton had warned of: "the next generation would not display the infinite patience we have had for half a century." After Stanton's death in 1902, and Anthony's passing in 1906, the suffrage movement split between the moderates and the radicals. Many members of the new generation found the National American of Suffrage Women Association (NASWA) too slow, too sedate. The head moderate was Carrie Chapman Catt who drew up what she called the "Winning Plan." It focused on winning suffrage state by state, and putting in place the machinery to lobby lawmakers and influence voters. It was issue based, a bipartisan approach to politics and an aversion to protests or flashy displays of any kind. The head radical was Alice Paul, who lived to create agitation and whose outrage fueled demonstrations designed to embarrass and anger the

Democrats in power for opposing suffrage. A generation younger than Catt she had learned her militant tactics from British suffragettes and Paul was brimming with an impatience that sprang from the conviction that her method was the "only method."

There was also an ever-growing group of men, members of the Men's League for Woman Suffrage, prominent reformers and activists, among them: George Foster Peabody, an eminent banker; Max Eastman, a professor at Columbia; Vassar president Henry Noble McCracken; historian Charles Beard, Rabbi Stephen Weiss and philosopher John Dewey. These men organized men's contingents to march in suffrage parades, held mass meetings for suffrage speakers, planned rallies and suffrage dinners.

In 1912, these men became part of massive suffrage parade. Organized by Mrs. O.H.P. Belmont, the former Alva Vanderbilt, nearing her sixtieth year and bored by her life in high society, she turned to the suffrage movement as a promising form of belligerency. And she was determined to give New York a spectacular demonstration of the movement's strength. Led by Inez Milholland, a renowned beauty, who sat upon a white horse, and marshaled by Mrs. Belmont, a long parade of white-clad feminists marched down Fifth Avenue to Washington Square—socialites, businesswomen, trade unionists, factory workers, housewives. Crowds lined the Avenue to see these fanatical "new women" who were undisturbed by ridicule, who brazenly asserted their equality with men.

The parade also included hundreds of men, members of the Men's League for Woman Suffrage. In a New York Times editorial, entitled "The Heroic Men," the League's part in the parade was noted:

The facts are all in print now about the masculine adherents of the women suffragists who will march in the parade tomorrow. There will be 800 of them surely. They will represent every trade and profession. The list includes bankers, manufacturers, students, librarians, dentists, musicians, bookkeepers, journalists, as well as dancing teachers, egg inspectors, capitalists, watchmen, ladies' waist makers and authors. A lawyer will carry the banner, and a fife and drum corps will head the division.

This is important news and not to be trifled with. The men who have professed to believe in woman suffrage have always been numerous. But these men are going to do more than profess; they are going to march before the eyes of the more or less unsympathetic multitude. It is one thing to sit on the platform and smile at a woman's meeting, quite another to march behind a gaudy banner to the inspiration of the squeaking fife, in order to indicate one's belief in the right of women to vote. The men will be closely scanned, but they will not mind that. They will be called endearing names by small boys on the sidewalk. But doubtless they will study to preserve their dignity. They will not march as well as the women. Only trained soldiers can compete with the amazons in keeping step. There must be strong inducement to make men march in a woman's parade . . . . But the majority must firmly believe in the righteousness of the cause, and also the value to it of their public appearance in line. They are courageous fellows. The march of the 800 may be renowned. We hope they will hold out, and we extend to all the 800 our sympathy and admiration.

Courageous fellows, yes, and strictly in the minority. At this parade and at others they were routinely jeered, sometimes even assaulted. Playwright George Middleton recalled that "the men every step of the two-mile walk had to submit to jeers, whistles, me-ows" and the taunts of the age which may seem strange to our ears but were insulting then, such as: "Take that handkerchief out of your cuff," "Oh, you gay deceiver," "You forgot to shave this morning," etc., etc. But not one man "deserted the ranks," Middleton reported proudly.

Those men who supported equal economic opportunities for women were occasional targets themselves, from firing to demotion. One West Virginia senator was threatened with dismissal as attorney for the United Fuel Gas Company if he did not change his vote on suffrage.

Wisconsin's Amos Wilder called the denial of woman suffrage:

The last form of caste lingering in the American system . . . . It is no answer to say that men vote for women. Why are not workingmen shut out from the franchise because employers vote for them? Why not debar left-handed men because right-handed men kindly offer to vote to relieve them of the duty and responsibility of voting? No class can get its fair representation by another class.

Arguments that voting would "unsex" women were countered by:

It doesn't unsex her to toil in a factory
  Minding the looms from the dawn til the night;
To deal with a schoolful of children refactory
  Doesn't unsex her in anyone's sight;
Work in a store—where her back aches inhumanly—
  Doesn't unsex her at all, you will note.

> *But think how exceedingly rough and unwomanly*
> *Woman would be if she happened to vote!*

Rabbi Stephen Weiss, one of the founders of the Men's League for Woman Suffrage, refuted the words of a member of the conservative clergy thusly:

An eloquent minister of the gospel says that women ought not to vote because suffrage is not a natural but a derived right. So is the right of your children to a common school education. So is our right to sanitary and police protection. But who will say that girls should be shut out from school or women from police protection because it is not a natural right?

Another great force opposed is Mr. Sleek Contented Conservatism . . . . He has stood in the way of every reform movement in history because his father did not believe in it and his grandfather never heard of it.

On March 3, 1913, the day before the inauguration of Woodrow Wilson, suffrage radical Alice Paul displayed her creation of eight thousand women in a parade that would start at the Capitol, march up Pennsylvania Avenue and end in a rally at the Hall of the Daughters of the American Revolution. Headed by the stunningly attractive Inez Milholland Boissevain (she had married in the past year) on a white horse, carrying a banner of purple, white and gold, Paul was sure that the excitement of this parade would capture the imagination of the suffrage movement and the country in contrast to the stern image of the early suffragists.

The nation's capital had never seen anything on the magnitude of the procession. Women from countries where suffrage had been granted (New Zealand, Finland) walked first. Next came the "pioneers," women now past middle age who had long agitated for the vote. Then, honoring the work of women in society: nurses in uniform, women farmers, factory workers, homemakers, librarians, college women in academic gowns. There were four mounted brigades, more than twenty floats and nine bands. Individual state delegations were followed by male supporters and, at the very end, a contingent of black women.

Although Paul had a parade permit, the men who had gathered surged onto Pennsylvania Avenue, heckling and jeering the women, making it almost impossible for the parade to pass. The police stood by and did nothing as the women were tripped and shoved, spat at, and had cigarette butts tossed at hem. The newspapers noted that the police seemed to enjoy and even participated in the melee. According to one newspaper account, two ambulances "came and went constantly for six hours, always impeded and at times actually opposed, so that doctor and driver literally had to fight their way to give succor to the injured."

Sedate Washington was appalled by the spectacle of drunken men shouting obscenities at women even though they were suffragists. There was a Congressional investigation, and a Senate committee held several days of hearings during which more than 150 witnesses recounted what they had seen. "There would be nothing like this happening if you had stayed at home," one senator chided the marchers. But the committee issued a blistering report on the failure of the police to protect the women, and the chief of police in the District of Columbia lost his job.

Early in 1914, Alice Paul began a concerted campaign lasting almost four years to force the administration and Congress to pass a suffrage amendment. Daily picketing at the

White House gate, carrying signs asking for the vote, holding the party in power responsible, causing embarrassment to Wilson who steadfastly refused to speak to them, led to extreme measures by the police. Suffragists were arrested for "unlawful assembly" or "obstructing traffic," sentenced to jail time and confined in unspeakable prison conditions: filthy cells with unwashed bedding, worm infested hominy or beans for food and little privacy. When suffragists were released, they resumed their pro-suffrage activities until they were again arrested and jailed.

The prison experience culminated in the "Night of Terror" on November 15, 1917, when Warden Whittaker at the workhouse in Virginia ordered his guards to teach a lesson to the suffragists imprisoned there. The prison guards wielding clubs beat the women, chained one to the cell bars high above her head, hurled one into a cell, smashing her head against an iron bed. There was grabbing, chocking, slamming, twisting and kicking the women. Instigating a hunger strike, Alice Paul was force-fed, having a tube inserted in one nostril when she refused to open her mouth. When news of the prison's conditions became known, the thirty suffrage prisoners were released on November 27 and 28.

The chairman of the House Committee on Suffrage, Andreus Aristides Jones of New Mexico, a longtime advocate of woman suffrage, set the date of January 10, 1918, for a vote. The suffrage amendment was passed by the House on that date by a vote of 274 to 136, the required two-thirds majority plus <u>one</u> vote to spare. Not until June 4, 1919, did the Senate pass the Nineteenth Amendment, now called the Susan B. Anthony Amendment, by a vote of 66 to 30; this was <u>two</u> more than needed.

To become law it had to be ratified by 36 of the 48 states. New Mexico was to be the 32nd state to ratify. Soon after the legislature convened February 16, 1920, the Senate voted 17-5 for ratification. But several House members had been convinced to renege on their promise to vote for ratification. Headlines in The New Mexican shamed the recalcitrant lawmakers by proclaiming: "Suffrage Totters On Edge of Defeat by Pledge-Breakers" and "Break Our Word to the Women of New Mexico—And Make the State a Laughing-Stock." Editorial comment in The New Mexican on the second day of wrangling warned: "If you turn down ratification you are not only violating a solemn pledge, making a political bonehead play and courting political ruin, but you are slapping in the face the splendid women of New Mexico and telling the world you don't think they're fit to have the ballot—or else you're afraid to let them have it."

On February 19, 1920, the vote was a landslide, with 36 voting for ratification and 10 against it.

Six months later Tennessee became the 36th state to ratify. The Tennessee Senate quickly ratified the amendment by a 25 to 6 margin, but for days the House was deadlocked. On August 18, 1920, the eyes of Americans everywhere were on Tennessee. Twice that day the bill had gone up for a vote. Twice the vote was tied: 48 - 48. Harry Burn at twenty-four was the youngest member of the House and had voted with the antis. The next morning the House was forced to vote again on the amendment. There was a letter in Harry Burn's pocket. It was from his mother. It said: "Dear son, be a good boy and vote for ratification." Harry Burn changed his "nay" to an "aye." And with that one vote American women were enfranchised!

On the eve of ratification one feminist newspaper had paid tribute to men's support:

It has been said that the suffragists have only themselves to thank for the victory that marks the end of a long struggle, but while the fight has been essentially woman's own, there have been hundreds of men throughout the country, in politics and out of politics, from the beginning of the fight to its end, who have so truly understood the aspirations that lay at the bottom of woman's endeavor, that they have stood shoulder to shoulder with her, helping in an earnest, dependable, generous, brotherly fashion, to bring about the things she sought . . . . There have been an ever-increasing number of true-hearted men . . . who have been the kind of suffragists to actually seek ways to help, and if occasion demanded, to make sacrifices for the cause.

The woman's suffrage movement, the political campaign to gain the vote, lasted 72 years from the first woman's convention in Seneca Falls until its culmination in 1920, with the passage of the Nineteenth Amendment to the Constitution of the United States. It was a war fought by hundreds of thousands of women and men, but without bullets or bombs, without taking a single life. Yet it was a war, won by the slimmest of margins. The challenges were great. The subject controversial, fueled by the ancient myth of woman's moral inferiority. American women, from their first gathering in convention, were to be faced with a volume of gynophobia, a true fear of women who now demanded rights that heretofore were enjoyed only by men.

Carrie Chapman Catt made this observation following the victory for the vote:

It is doubtful if any man, even among the suffrage men, ever realized what the suffrage struggle came to mean for women before the end was allowed in America, How much time and patience, how much work, energy and aspiration, how much faith, how much hope, how much despair went into it. It leaves its mark on one, such a struggle. It fills the days and rules the nights. Working, eating, drinking, sleeping, it is there.

But woman's struggle for equality, political and otherwise did not end with the passage of the Nineteenth Amendment.

In 1924, Doris Stevens said: *There is not a state in the Union in which men and women live under equal protection of the law . . . . Woman is still conceived to be in subject to and under the control of the husband if married or the male members of the family if unmarried.*

In 1925, Crystal Eastman wrote:

What is this problem of woman's freedom? It seems to be this: how to arrange the world so that women can be human beings, with a chance to exercise their infinitely varied gifts in infinitely varied ways, instead of being destined by accident of their sex to one field of activity—housework and child-raising. And second, if and when they choose housework and child-raising, to have that occupation recognized by the world as work, requiring a definite economic reward and not merely entitling the performer to be dependent on some man.

Suffrage did not bring equality in the workplace, it did not end academic sexism nor improve woman's economic equality. There is the seemingly never-ending struggle to allow woman to have control over her own body and to be protected from male violence and rape. It becomes a matter of constant vigilance to keep from losing rights which have been gained. Supreme Court Judge Harry Blackmun cogently observed in 1989, concerning the weakening of Roe v. Wade:

"The signs are evident and very ominous, and a chill wind blows."

To repeat the words of Louise Otto written in 1849, holding their truth for today and for generations to come:

The history of all times, and of today especially, teaches that . . . Women will be forgotten if they forget to think about themselves.

It is as true today as it was so long ago. Women must think about themselves, ensuring that the woman's vote does indeed express their desires for whatever changes they deem necessary and that it prevents further erosion of rights fought for in the past. They must fight continually for their rights and watch constantly for fear those rights will be taken away while their backs are turned or just when they begin to feel safe and comfortable. Gynephobia still lurks in the hearts and minds of some men and, unfathomably, in some women. And the myth of Eve still resonates surreptitiously from boardroom, legislative chamber, and pulpit.

Marilyn A. as Susan B.
Portrait by Dorothy Hoard

Marilyn Adams is an educator, holding degrees in English and history; an actor with a lifetime of theatrical experiences, beginning with Children's Theatre, with an occasional foray into regional and community productions, culminating in one-woman shows as a Chautauqua Scholar for the New Mexico Humanities Council, portraying Susan B. Anthony, Victoria Woodhull and Eleanor Roosevelt throughout the state. As a writer she has scripted two historical endeavors: <u>An Improper Woman</u>, a dramatic survey of the nineteenth woman's movement and <u>Men Who Stood With Women for Equality</u>, highlighting pro-feminist men of the nineteenth and early twentieth centuries.

A founding member of the Santa Fe Mad Hatters, easily recognizable by her "flying nun" hats, she conducts walking tours of historic Santa Fe.

As a performer and historian, eager to impart the history of woman's struggle for civil, social and legal equality, Marilyn is uniquely qualified to help young people as well as those of older generations to understand the importance of the battle for equality, every woman's right to enjoy what is due every human being.